Julius Lo

Public Speaking

– Speaking like a Professional –

How to become a better speaker, present yourself convincingly and increase your self-confidence through successful communication

First published in Germany in October 2018
By Julius Loewenstein

Original First Edition USA: April 2019
Copyright © 2019 Julius Conrad Loewenstein

Independently published

Paperback: 978 1093 69996 8

Print / Delivery: Amazon or subsidiary

www.julius-loewenstein.com

Content

Foreword

Why a book on public speaking?

In today's world, **the art of speaking** is gaining more and more importance. Increasingly, we are faced with situations in which it is important
to speak freely in front of an audience. Whether in a professional or private context: For many people, this poses a challenge - irrespective of
whether it is a speech at a family celebration, a price negotiation at a car
dealer or a presentation in front of employees.

Especially in professional life, self-confident talking is more important
than ever before. If you want to be successful these days, you have to
communicate credibly and convince your fellow human beings of yourself. Those who cannot sell themselves and their ideas properly will not
achieve lasting success in professional life. This applies equally to the
self-employed, entrepreneurs and employees.

But also in everyday life it is necessary to master the art of speech and
to use it profitably for oneself and one's interests. Those who speak authentically and self-confidently and argue wisely achieve more than those who do not. When looking for a partner, planning an upcoming family holiday or simply selecting a restaurant - if we really want to assert
our interests and gain more decision-making power, there is no way
around using the power of rhetoric to convince people sustainably.

Which messages you convey to your audience depends to a large
extent on how you use your body and voice, but also on what you say -
and of course how you say something. Make every effort to convey the
messages you want to convey to the audience. Messages that are presented in a confident manner and help you get what you want. In this case,
the audience is the customer, the boss or the employee, your partner,
your children or your parents. Or whoever: Actually, all the people you

talk to are part of your audience. And this audience needs to be convinced - of both your personality and your ideas.

Your appearance, i.e. your perceived competence, is decisive for success and failure in professional life. It goes without saying that the content of what has been said must also be correct. Whether you are taken seriously, or whether you are perceived: A direct result of verbal and non-verbal communication - and the quality of your presentation.

This book summarizes the most important rhetoric strategies of the last 2500 years to ensure that you succeed in giving professional speeches in the future, impressing your audience with powerful arguments and winning the hearts of your listeners. Aristotle, Jesus Christ and Barack Obama already benefited from these methods, making them the greatest speakers in human history.

Maybe you won't be a great speaker like they were. But certainly the strategies mentioned here in the book will help you communicate more effectively in everyday life and at work, increase your perceived competence, appear self-confident, find the right words at the right time and, above all, inspire and enthral people.

In addition, you will learn valuable tactics on how to control conversations and assert your interests using convincing rhetoric. You will also learn how to behave in the context of professional negotiations, meetings and presentations and how to present yourself competently. This book is intended to help you better achieve your professional and personal goals by enhancing the quality of your communication.

Thanks to the strategies presented in this book, you will gain new insights. Insights that form the basis for learning and applying the art of speech and thus improving your professional relationships, but also for convincing people of your ideas in a private context - thanks to good rhetoric.

Julius C. Loewenstein, Hamburg 2018

Introduction

What you need to know in advance

To become a good speaker, you need to be familiar with the basics of rhetoric. And in order to understand the basics, you should first know what rhetoric means and involves.

The term rhetoric originates from the Greek and means *the art of speaking* or *the art of eloquence*. Those who master this art of speech have the power to inspire people and give speeches during which the audience listens attentively and ultimately remembers the content. With good rhetoric you can convince the audience of your ideas and even arouse feelings in the listener.

Rhetoric is the art of effectively speaking and convincing. Standing in front of an audience during a lecture or presentation (monologue), as well as in conversation, in a negotiation or a dispute (dialogical).

Rhetoric is science and art form at the same time. The scientific part deals with the way of an effective lecture and focuses on the methods and stylistic devices of a good speech. The theoretical knowledge and the analysis of successful speeches and speakers are in the foreground. Among other things, the following questions will be answered: How do effective speeches work? How are they structured?

But rhetoric is also an art form, since creating a speech is a creative act, similar to a music or theatre play. This includes delivering the speech to an audience, an act that requires rhetorical talent, presence and charisma to decisively influence the end result. So the art of rhetoric is to convey a message so impressively that you win the audience over.

But what does that mean for you? After all, you want to inform your audience about a certain problem. Or trigger emotions in people and inspire others for your cause. Or do you prefer to gain an upper hand during conflicts and resolve them in way that benefits you?

In this guide, I will demonstrate how you can achieve all this. It is a guide that goes beyond theoretical explanations. A guide that provides you with the necessary strategies in a practical, clear and precise way enabling you to communicate successfully, act confidently and finally win over your fellow human beings and convince them of your beliefs. This book covers everything worth knowing about rhetoric, from building a good speech to the twelve steps *"from idea to lecture"*.

Thanks to the knowledge conveyed here, you will also learn how to present yourself confidently during the lecture and how to present your interests credibly - so that in the end you will not only speak more frequently in everyday life and at work, but also assert your opinion more frequently.

However, in order to achieve this goal, you must also apply the tips that are abundantly available in this book. The methods that are formulated have been designed in a way to be easily implemented in everyday life and to best serve you in enhancing your communication skills. After all, you only learn to speak by speaking. Therefore, this book focuses on practice rather than theory - or in other words - the theoretical foundations are transformed into practical recommendations.

In this book I provide you with practical contents based on my own experiences, on the many books I have read and studied on the subject of rhetoric, or on analyses I have made of countless great speeches. To share with you the strategies that have been tried and tested in ancient Greece, but also methods that are used today and that are useful in all areas of life.

This book is intended for beginners, experienced speakers as well as professionals. Regardless of your rhetoric level, or how good (or bad) your rhetorical skills are, you will almost certainly discover advice here that you may not have known before and that will help you improve your art of speaking.

If you use the knowledge gained from this book profitably for yours-elf, you can achieve great as well as small successes. You can use this knowledge to become immortal in people's minds, to impress your em-ployees or to apply it in negotiations - so that you can easily achieve your professional as well as your private goals. It's all in your own hands.

However, the key to success lies - as so often - in action. Take action. Apply the knowledge. And you will be richly rewarded.

I hope you enjoy reading this book and gain valuable insights.

Sincerely yours,

Julius Loewenstein

First Things First

In the following chapters you will learn the basics of rhetoric. You will gain knowledge about beginner's mistakes and learn how to avoid them, what kinds of speech exist, on what occasions they are used and what the structure of a good speech should look like. I will also show you how to structure your speech using a simple strategy.

5 Beginner's Mistakes you Should Better Avoid

The beginner's mistakes described in the following are introduced with a short case study to better understand the concept. The examples all represent everyday situations in professional life, but this does not mean that they are not applicable to everyday life.

---

1. BEGINNER'S MISTAKE:
You say something, but it does not correspond to your feelings.

Max is in the middle of an important sales talk that he has been preparing for for weeks. He has to win over the potential customer and convince him of the attractiveness of his company's products to ensure that the customer buys the products. If the customer accepts the offer, it will be a great success for him and his company. If the customer refuses, Max will face difficult times. The pressure is correspondingly high. He's nervous ...

Max begins his presentation as follows:

"I am delighted to be able to present our services to you today. You'll be thrilled."

But his voice sounds completely different. The tone of his voice expresses fear and nervousness and does not give the impression that Max is happy. His movements are hesitant and indecisive.

He seems insecure and his counterpart notices that. Will the customer be enthusiastic after such an entry? I don't think so.

I will later explain in this book how to get your nervousness under control. But the point now is that you shouldn't start saying something you don't feel. Of course, it's well meant when you say you're happy. But this joy should also be real. Authentic. It is important that you convey credibility right from the start and do not stifle trust from the outset.

Humans have an unmistakable sixth sense for sensing moods. We can read the emotions of others in a fraction of a second based on their tone of voice, body language and facial expression. When the words express something other than how they are spoken, we do not let ourselves be deceived and instinctively distrust the person.

What we say must be brought into harmony with our feelings. If you say that yu are happy, you should also sense the feeling of joy. If, on the other hand, you are stressed or nervous and then say that you are cheerful, this has a negative effect not only on your standing. As a result, you will be considered untrustworthy and will lose the trust of the listener.

But even in another form this is not good for you: You only become more stressed and nervous. After all, your emotional state does not correspond to what you say and an inner disharmony develops - which only makes the whole thing worse.

Of course, it is best if you develop a feeling of joy for yourself in advance and introduce the lecture with enthusiasm that will infect your audience. But you also have to convey this feeling authentically.

What can help develop this feeling? Imagine a happy ending. Think of the beautiful feeling when you pass your enthusiasm on to your listeners and get yourself into this emotional state before it starts. Immerse yourself in the feeling of joy right from the start and you will inevitably feel better. Imagine the success already - as pictorial as possible.

Then it will certainly be easier for you to really enjoy yourself and convince your audience with this honest pleasure.

Therefore, the first tip is to avoid beginner's mistakes:

Just say things you really mean and feel.
Credibility is the key.

---

2. BEGINNER'S MISTAKE:
Too many excuses!

Anna is in the middle of a presentation standing in front of her department. She is supposed to present the business figures of the last year to her employees. But before she starts, she introduces her lecture as follows:

"Ladies and gentlemen, I am sorry that the slides have not turned out well. Unfortunately, I didn't have much time because of my children, so I had to finish my work quickly last night. Besides, I have a little cold. Excuse my voice, please. I hope you don't mind."

You see what this is all about? Too many excuses weaken a speech. Anna creates the impression of unprofessionalism and impairs a sovereign appearance. By drawing attention at the very beginning to the fact that everything went wrong and that the poor quality of the lecture was therefore to be excused, she seems more like a flag in the wind than a confident speaker.

Her audience would probably not have noticed the inadequacies of the lecture at all, nor would they have felt disturbed by them. Due to the many apologies and the meaningless excuses Anna unnecessarily focuses on those inadequacies, which actually shouldn't (should) carry much weight.

She also burdens her audience with the responsibility of accepting her apologies for her mistakes. That's not smart!

The lecture itself requires the full attention of your audience. If you direct the focus on your mistakes beforehand, it will be more difficult for the audience to take seriously what you are going to say and it will also be harder for you to present yourself professionally.

You'd better forgo apologies. Accept your mistakes, but do not explicitly point them out to your audience. Don't look for reasons why things didn't work out.

"The quality of the slides is sufficient to show you the essentials."

"Cold or no cold - we should definitely take a look at the quarterly figures."

**Demonstrate sovereignty and be professional –
no one needs apologies.**

3. BEGINNER'S MISTAKE:
The „Know-it-all"

Imagine the following scenery: Robert successfully applied the previous two tips and feels fit to give a lecture in front of 50 people in his company. The topic: Chances of digitization. The presentation runs like clockwork. The audience is interested in the topic. Robert has done everything right - until a critical question is asked at the end:

"Do you know the recently published Stanford University study on the impact of artificial intelligence on consolidating labor markets?"

Robert is confused - but does not want to appear unprepared. After all, he has to convince people of his knowledge! Although he has never heard of the study and does not understand the question at all, Robert answers arrogantly:

"Yes. I'm very familiar with the study. It shows the impact on labor markets, which is indeed negative rather than positive, and ..."

The questioner smells a rat:

"Are you sure? The study clearly shows that artificial intelligence creates new, creative jobs by transforming the old ones. That's actually good!"

Ouch! Embarrassing! He went in half-cocked pretending to know the study. Even if this faux pas is not so bad (Who knows this study?), the effect is fatal. No matter how good the speech may have been, such a blunder can ruin everything. The audience is insecure - the speaker doesn't seem to be as competent as originally assumed.

This mistake is typical of those who have given some good speeches and thereby acquired a certain rhetorical confidence. A safety measure that must be preserved at all costs! Just don't show any weakness! Right?

In this case, the mistaken belief arises that a gap in knowledge would destroy a speech that has been delivered safely. We believe that we have to be smarter than our audience and that the impression of stupidity and unknowingness may arise if we cannot answer a question confidently. But keep in mind: In the above example, 50 people sit in the room - fifty heads dispose of more knowledge than one. Of course, the presenter should know his subject better than his audience (otherwise he would not need to give a lecture).

Be aware that your audience includes people who are also experts in certain subject areas that may overlap with what you are talking about.

Don't try to fool your audience - it can go awry! Try to be modest and admit your lack of knowledge.

This may sound like a contradiction considering the previous chapter. Look at it this way: We have to be honest with our audience and admit our lack of knowledge in case we don't know or understand something. At the same time, however, it is necessary to be certain of what we know and what we have finally prepared ourselves for and to make the most of that knowledge. It is better to include the questioner in your presentation and link his or her information with yours. This is evidence of strength and authenticity.

An optimal answer in our case example could be as follows:

"Unfortunately, I'm not familiar with this study. Can you tell us a bit about it? We can certainly integrate the information into the topic and gain a new valuable perspective from it."

The questioner tells what he knows. Robert thanks for the suggestion and can then establish a meaningful link between the supplemented information and his presentation. In addition to enriching the content, the audience automatically perceives him as more competent. Robert is open to new ideas and shows in a professional way that he doesn't know everything either. This creates valuable sympathy.

If there is one thing you don't know, it's no big deal.
Use new information to add depth to your speech.

4. BEGINNER'S MISTAKE:
Choosing the Wrong Words!

At his company's summer party, Nick wants to give a memorable farewell speech for a loyal colleague who was very close to him and is now retiring.

"Ladies and gentlemen, I will try not to create a mood of mourning. Mr. Goodman has been more than just another employee. He has also been a friend to all of us. He has made sure that no boredom has ever arisen in his office and has spared no effort to get the department out of the dark times. Mr. Goodman has always been a hard worker. And for that, we especially appreciate him ... "

Phew. What kind of atmosphere does the speech create? Grief ... boredom ... difficult times ... Despite the well-meant words, Mr. Goodman will not have the feeling that he has been a valued employee and friend. Nick does not create a pleasant mood and it is doubtful whether Mr. Goodman will enjoy his farewell. Nick, his listeners and especially Mr. Goodman will have certainly not imagined it this way.

The words we choose generate either a positive, or a negative, or a neutral effect, which trigger certain emotional states in the listener. We should be aware of that. Words are faster than sentences. We first hear and understand individual words before we relate them to each other and understand the actual meaning of the sentence.

Therefore negations should always be used with caution. Their message reaches the listener later than the single word. Words and core statement should coincide with each other and therefore phrases like *"I will try not to let a mood of mourning arise"* cause the exact opposite of what one wanted to achieve with one's speech. And what do they produce? Mourning.

It is advisable to select only the words that trigger the desired mood in the listener. The words should match the intention of the speech and support, underline, underpin its message - you name it.

Imagine that we would associate an image with each word, i.e. associate the word with a visual idea. Isn't it wise for this image to support the message we want to convey? For example, if you want to praise someone, avoid the phrase *"not bad"* and say *"well done"* instead. Or replace *"it doesn't do you any harm"* with *"you'll benefit from it!"*

Once you have understood and internalized the concept, you will be able to reach people better with your words and address the feelings that you would like to arouse in your audience.

Here is another alternative to the above farewell speech:

"Ladies and gentlemen, Mr. Goodman, a committed, motivated and cheerful member of our company, is now entering his well-earned retirement. Thanks to Mr. Goodman's ambitious nature, he has always contributed to the company's success and thanks to his open-mindedness we have enjoyed many wonderful moments together at work. On behalf of the entire company, I would like to thank you, Mr. Goodman, for being part of our unique team. Thank you very much."

As you can see, the speech now has a completely different quality compared to the first one. Nick addresses the right feelings of the audience and will certainly delight Mr. Goodman very much.

Inspire with the right words. Words make the difference!

5. BEGINNER'S MISTAKE:
Filled pauses such as "um" or "uh"

"Um ... I'm glad you're all here. Today I would like to introduce you to our new marketing strategy that we created last week. Therefore, I have prepared a small presentation, um ... which will show you the whole thing. So, uh ... the strategy is, of course, to spend more money on advertising."

The most widespread and perhaps even most critical beginner's mistakes, which sabotage a good speech and a self-confident appearance, are the constant hesitation phenomena such as *"um"* or *"uh"*, which many people like to use when talking. A speech should be impulsive, dynamic and thrilling, inspire the audience, facilitate listening for the audience!

But what is the final effect of these hesitation phenomena? They ruin everything.

Those who constantly and regularly repeat *"um"* and *"uh"* must not expect their audience to follow them attentively. The lecture will be tough. And when it's particularly extreme, some bored listeners quickly start counting the number of your *"ums"* und *"uhs"* instead of paying attention to the content.

If you need a break to briefly consider what you want to say next, then take that break! Thinking works even when we are silent. We don't have to produce a stupid sound such as *"um"*.

Many people are afraid of such pauses for thought. Beginners consider this a disturbing interruption that worries the listener and fear losing attention when "nothing at all" happens for a moment. The opposite is true. Pauses in speech maintain the listener's attention and arouse curiosity. They will make you curious about what the speaker will say next.

Effectively used pauses provide the audience with time to process what has already been said for a moment and therefore have the advantage of highlighting important statements. This makes such pauses a powerful tool that helps listeners remember the speech for a long time to come. A short pause in speech usually doesn't occur to the audience as long as the speaker might think.

Of course, it takes a little courage and training to stop the hesitation phenomena such as *"um"* and learn to use the pauses correctly. To make this easier for you, I will show you the two different types of speech pauses that need to be distinguished:

Inter-pauses (pauses between sentences) give the audience time to reflect. As just described, these types of pauses have the purpose of understanding what has just been said and processing the information. In addition, these pauses give the opportunity to search for questions if the statement has become unclear. If the inter-pauses are longer, these questions are also asked.

Intra-pauses (pauses within the sentence) make the audience think ahead. They arouse curiosity about what's coming and create suspense. In such moments, the attention of the audience increases, which is the reason why intra-pauses should always be placed before your most important statements. Eye contact, position changes, supportive gestures and a change of tone particularly unfold the power of these pauses.

Let us apply the newly acquired knowledge to our case study again.

"I'm glad you're all here. ... [pause] Today I would like to introduce you to our new marketing strategy, which we created last week. ... [pause] For this purpose I have prepared a small presentation, which shall simply show you the whole thing. ... [pause] The strategy ... [intra-pause] is to spend more money on advertising."

A simple formula with a strong effect. Make sure you use pauses for your presentation and place them cleverly to create drama and tension.

**Replace expressions such as "um" with well-placed pauses.
Your audience will be grateful.**

5 Beginner's Mistakes You Should Better Avoid

1. BEGINNER'S MISTAKE:
You say something, but it does not correspond to your feelings.

Anything you say should be consistent with your feelings. Say only things that correspond to your emotions so that the audience considers you credible and your words meaningful.

Say only things you really mean and feel.
Credibility is the key.

2. BEGINNER'S MISTAKE:
Too many excuses!

If your talk is not optimal, that's no reason to worry. Instruct your audience, but not explicitly on the mistakes. This testifies to sovereignty.

Demonstrate sovereignty and be professional -
no one needs apologies.

3. BEGINNER'S MISTAKE:
The „Know-it-all"

Be honest with your audience and admit your lack of knowledge or understanding. Give your audience the opportunity to participate actively and enrich your presentation with new ideas and information.

If you do not know a detail, don't worry.
Use new information to add depth to your speech.

(Summary)

4. BEGINNER'S MISTAKE:
Choosing the Wrong Words!

Pay attention to the words you choose. Try using individual words to awaken images and associations in the audience that serve your purpose and create an appropriate atmosphere.

Impress with the right words. Words make the difference!

5. BEGINNER'S MISTAKE:
Filled pauses such as "um" or "uh"

Instead of stretching an *"um"* for the 34th time, you should include pauses in your speech because they produce tension, provide time for reflection and make it easier for listeners to stay alert. The appearance will become more sovereign if you know how to use the effect of pauses.

Replace your "um" with speech pauses.
Your audience will be grateful.

Three Types of Speech:
Are You a Mentor, Doer or Muse?

Before you begin to speak in front of an audience, you should know *why* you are speaking. What are you trying to achieve with this speech? What would you like to pass on to the audience? Do you want to inform the audience, convince them or create a certain mood?

A distinction must be made between three types of speech. Or as the father of rhetoric, Aristotle, once put it two and a half thousand years ago in ancient Greece:

> *"... from this it follows that there are three divisions of oratory -*
> *(1) political, (2) forensic, and (3) the ceremonial oratory of display."*
>
> **Aristotle**

Depending on the occasion and the audience, we can choose between three ways of persuasion:

1) **the informative speech (also factual lecture)**
2) **the persuasive speech (opinion speech)**
3) **the occasional speech**

Knowing the individual genres of speech and their characteristics and properties and being able to distinguish between them is essential for a rhetorically confident performance. It should be mentioned that the three types of speech can also overlap and that mixed forms are possible.

A good speech requires good preparation. And in order to be able to prepare a speech optimally, one should be aware of the purpose of the speech. Once you have defined this goal for yourself, the above forms of speech will help you take the right path to achieve the desired result and deliver the right messages to the audience.

The Informative Speech (Mentor)

The informative speech, also called factual presentation, is primarily intended to present and clarify facts. It serves to convey information and knowledge to the audience and to sum up content in a clear, understandable, objective and factual way. The purpose of an informative speech is to address the mind of the listener and to educate the audience in a certain way.

The focus in this case is on logical reasoning. You try to convince the listener with solid evidence - be it numbers, data, facts or even conclusive arguments.

You try to convince the listener with solid evidence - be it numbers, data, facts or even conclusive arguments.

Important: The speaker does not express his opinion. This form of speech focuses on an objective presentation of the facts. The speaker may express his own thoughts on the subject, but should clearly separate his views from the content. The lecture itself is free of judgement and the lecturer must take this into account.

When to apply?

- **The main focus of professional or scientific lectures** is on information.

- The informative speech is also used in the context of **school and vocational education.** The teacher or trainer passes on information to his students.

- The various **types of reports** also focus on passing on information (weather report, media report, management report, annual report). See Reporting.

The Persuasive Speech (Doer)

A persuasive speech is probably the most important form of speech of the three forms. It is also called an opinion speech and is used almost everywhere: whether in a professional or business context, or also in political and social contexts.

The aim is to convince people or motivate them to take a certain action in order to assert their interests. Therefore, it is impossible to imagine private life and everyday business without the persuasive speech.

We must constantly convince our fellow human beings of our ideas, and for this purpose it is necessary to present one's own opinion attractively and to win over the audience both logically and emotionally.

The persuasive speech, as already mentioned, is aimed at achieving a certain goal. This is predominantly done by means of clear expressions, which are accompanied by linguistic and rhetorical means.

Especially regarding this form of speech, the speaker must convey credibility in order to win the trust of the audience. Without the trust of the audience, he cannot convey his message to them.

The explanations are limited to the essentials and factual information is used sparingly to ensure that it does not distract from the objective. However, figures, data and facts can be used to support the opinion expressed by the speaker.

The argumentation is usually one-sided and counter-arguments are only used to refute them - as a result a clear evaluation of the facts can be ascertained in the persuasive speech. At the end of the speech, an appeal is made to the audience.

The persuasive speech primarily addresses the will and feelings of the listeners in order to motivate them to act or to accept the speaker's point of view.

When to apply?

- In everyday **professional life**, the persuasive speech definitely represents an advantage. In the context of salary negotiations, meetings, meetings, product presentations, sales talks or small talk the opinion speech usually pays off.

- In the **social sphere** we often observe persuasive speeches. Politicians and generally persons holding (high) offices often have to prove their rhetorical abilities every day anew in form of persuasive speeches in order to be elected or to secure the support of the people.

- We should also master the art of the persuasive speech in our **private lives**. Whether we make big decisions (What should we name our child?) or small decisions (Where should we eat?), we need to be trained to effectively express our ideas so that our projects will be supported by others.

The Occasional Speech (Muse)

The occasional speech is usually given on special occasions. It is applied when a certain occasion is to be appreciated, which is particularly the case with ceremonial speeches and funeral orations.

The speaker is expected to capture the mood (joy, sadness, departure) appropriate to the occasion and to address the feelings of the audience and make the audience reflect on the event. Inspiring, entertaining, touching - that is the meaning of an occasional speech.

Frequently, inexperienced speakers use empty phrases. It is therefore advisable to use linguistic images, because images have a higher expressiveness than words. Stories and anecdotes should therefore be incorporated into the occasional speech, they bring the speech to life and move the audience.

The occasional speech should be short and captivating. The audience expects you to inspire them and trigger their emotions. It is advantageous if you put yourself in the mood that you would like to evoke in the audience. This allows you to perform credibly and makes it easier to convey your message to the audience and capture the hearts of the listeners.

When to apply?

- Occasional speeches are mainly given when congratulations are expressed at **celebrations and festivities** such as birthdays or a wedding.

- **Sad events**, such as the death of a beloved and esteemed fellow human being, can also be the occasion for an occasional speech.

- **Farewell and welcoming speeches** by new or old employees, guests or chairmen are also suitable occasions for occasional speeches.

- **Honors such as anniversaries or certain merits** of teams or individuals are also a popular way to honor a particular achievement or event with a successful speech.

Make sure you have a clear picture of what you are talking about and what your intentions are. Do you want to inform, convince or inspire?

On the basis of this you will select the appropriate form of speech and learn to master it (the practical tools for this will be explained to you later). This chapter aims to provide you with a more theoretical understanding of the different types of speeches.

It is important to note that you should not commit to just one of the forms of speech. In order to really master the art of rhetoric, it is advisable not only to know all three forms of speech, but also - more or less - to be able to master them. If you use all three forms of speech regularly, you will not only enhance your overall communication skills, but also improve your individual forms (mentor, doer, muse).

Being able to deliver a good speech and inspire audiences, whether the focus of the speech is on information sharing, persuasion, or emotion triggering, makes a truly good speaker.

Even if you specialize in scientific lectures, you should be able to give a suitable speech at your sister's wedding.

Besides, it can never hurt to know how to respond to the listener's emotions, no matter what situation you find yourself in and what kind of speaker you "actually" are. Besides, it can never hurt to know how to respond to the listener's emotions, no matter what situation you find yourself in and what kind of speaker you actually are.

Learn to master all three forms of speech. Expand your knowledge and skills by practicing strategies of how to inform, persuade and inspire people to make sure that you are always capable of impressing the audience. No matter what the occasion. Because that's what makes a good speaker special: Flexibility.

3 Types of Speech: Are you a Mentor, Doer or Muse?

The Informative Speech (Mentor)

The primary purpose of the informative speech is to present information objectively. It is helpful to use numbers, data and facts. The logical and rational examination of the facts plays a central role, hence the name Logos according to Aristotle.

Goal: Teaching and arguing, imparting knowledge

How? With sound and objectively value-free arguments that appear logical and, if necessary, are substantiated.

The Persuasive Speech (Doer)

The persuasive speech is characterized by the fact that the speech is directed towards a certain goal. As a rule, this goal is to convince the listener of the speaker's views and values and, in some cases, to motivate him to take a certain action. The facts are clearly assessed and evaluated so that they serve the interests of the speaker. (Ethos)

Goal: Winning and delighting, convincing the audience of yourself and your cause.

How? Rhetorical stylistic devices can help to influence the listener consciously and subconsciously.

(Summary)

The Occasional Speech (Muse)

Occasional speeches are used for example to celebrate a person's life, to mourn a person's loss, or to honor a person or an event. The aim is to capture the mood and move the audience with emotional words and lively language. The speech is usually short and captivating, the speaker awakens the listener's feelings. (Pathos)

Goal: Touching and moving, triggering feelings and stimulating reflection.

How? Anecdotes, personal stories, humor, quotations, linguistic imagery.

3 Parts – Speech Outline:
Structuring the Speech

"The speaker needs to pay attention to three things: what he wants to present, in what order and in what way."
Marcus Tullius Cicero (106 BC - 43 BC)

A clear outline is a key prerequisite for the success of any speech. It helps organize thoughts and ensures that the speech is congruent. In order to prepare a speech optimally, you need a meaningful outline.

It offers you a clear structure, which you only have to follow during the preparation and during the presentation - which will make your speech a lot easier.

From school we still know the classic three-way division. Every (reasonable) lecture is structured according to this setup:

> i)   **Introduction**
>
> ii)   **Main part**
>
> iii)   **Conclusion**

This standard scheme has been used since early antiquity and has proven successful in many respects. Whether speeches, presentations, books, court statements or newspaper commentaries - interpersonal communication is largely based on this tripartite division.

In the following we will take a closer look at the three parts. The focus is clearly on the introduction.

The Introduction

The introduction is the most important part of a speech. If you introduce your presentation correctly and establish a good connection to the audience right from the start, you will secure the attention of the audience and create a stable basis for a convincing performance.

The introduction is about more than just establishing the first contact with the audience and welcoming each other. The first words of a speech can be decisive for success or failure.

You should therefore reflect very carefully on how you introduce yourself, which words you will use first and how you want to introduce the topic. There are a few things you should keep in mind. Let's start with the welcome.

Welcome and Salutation

Always welcome your listeners! I wish I didn't have to draw attention to that necessity. Unfortunately, it is actually the case that - although it seems to be taken for granted - many people skip it, ignore it or simply forget to welcome the audience at all. Whether it's excitement or lack of experience, I don't know. In any case, it is absolutely essential to welcome your audience.

The welcoming of guests (your listeners are, so to speak, your guests) is an expression of respect in accordance with social norms and certain values such as courtesy.

Always start your lecture by addressing the audience appropriately. A brief salutation and a friendly greeting represent your first chance to connect with the audience. Imagine that there is an invisible barrier between you and your listeners that you have to overcome as quickly as possible to feel safe while speaking. The right salutation is the best way to get started.

The best-case scenario for this depends on the occasion and the audience. The usual salutation *"Ladies and Gentlemen"* is quite impersonal - but you can't go wrong with it. However, the listeners will feel more addressed if you refer more specifically to those present.

Examples:

"Dear employees" or "Dear colleagues"

"Dear guests"

"Dear fellow citizens"

"Dear club members"

If outstanding personalities are present, they must also be addressed by name and title (or both):

"Dear Mrs President, Ladies and Gentlemen"

"Dear Mayor Fuchs"

"Dear Members of the Supervisory Board"

Check in advance who is to be greeted, but avoid long lists of names. Keep the salutation short and concise. All those present should get the feeling that they are appreciated for their presence. Communicate this feeling by means of a clear and personal form of address. Afterwards you can greet your audience with one of the following phrases.

A classical phrase that is suitable for all types of speech.

"I'm very pleased to welcome you today."

Are you dealing with a large crowd?

"I am happy to see you in such great numbers. Thank you."

It is a special occasion and there are well-known guests in the audience.

"It's a great honor to welcome you here today."

The importance of the first sentence

After the salutation it is important to successfully introduce the topic. The introductory sentence after the greeting is decisive as to whether and how much interest the audience will show later. The effect of this first movement must capture the attention of the audience from the very beginning and - if appropriate - arouse the enthusiasm of the audience.

How you manage it is up to you. In any case, the first sentence must introduce the topic, be easy to understand and affect the audience.

Demonstrate to your listeners that the topic you are presenting is related to them. And that applies to all kinds, whether you talk about deforestation or present the latest technological changes in your product at a meeting - people will listen to you only marginally if you don't make them feel the topic is interesting for them.

Or do you think your audience will be moved by your presentation if you start reading the quarterly figures immediately? Be so kind and give your listeners a reason why they should pay attention to you.

In case you want to draw attention to a global problem and address the sense of responsibility of the audience:

"In the next few minutes, I will present a problem that has reached alarming dimensions / that concerns us all."

And here is a template if you want to convince someone in your professional environment, be it employees or customers:

"I'll show you possible solutions to the problem you have been struggling with for a long time."

"The model I want to present to you today can be of great help to us to tackle our future tasks."

You may already notice that the primary point is to put yourself in the listener's shoes and, at best, to offer him solutions to his problems. Because aren't our problems exactly what concerns us the most? What are you more likely to focus your attention on? That a tree toppled in front of your house or that there was another famine in Africa?

Studies have repeatedly confirmed that the first kind of news, the toppled tree in front of our house, affects us *much* more than something - tragic, yes - that happened far away from our centre of life.

Help your audience by providing solutions to their problems. Use this perspective the next time you speak to an audience or a person in general. Put yourself in your listener's shoes. What's he interested in? What are his biggest worries? Many untrained speakers make the mistake of talking too much about themselves and their own problems.

Professional speakers, on the other hand, put themselves in the other person's position and gain the attention of their listeners not least because of this.

How to introduce yourself the right way

It often happens that the speaker has to introduce himself. This is particularly the case with lectures. The principle behind this is obvious: the listener first wants to know who is standing in front of him before the lecture begins and things get serious.

The good thing about it is that the lecturer (usually) decides what the audience should learn about him. Accordingly, the lecturer can compile the information in such a way that it serves the purpose of the lecture.

The scope of the introduction depends entirely on the respective situation. If you give a speech about your life's work, your personal presentation will of course require more time and background information than if you give a lecture about steam navigation in the 19th century in front of your audience.

The spectrum of possible information ranges from the name, the origin, the company represented by you to the current role and a short curriculum vitae. In principle, however, the following applies: Keep your personal details as brief as possible. Remember what was mentioned in the previous subchapter! The listeners have not necessarily come for your sake (unless you are a celebrity or otherwise an important personality), but mainly because of what you have to say about the subject.

Ideally, you can use personal information to link it to the topic and make a successful transition to the main part.

For example, a suitable introduction might look like this (after you have adequately welcomed the audience):

"When I was seven years old, my parents moved with me to the United States. I couldn't speak a single word of English, but within a very short time I was able to speak the language fluently. My parents, on the other hand, had difficulties mastering the language for a long time and have maintained their Italian accent to this day. In this lecture I would like to give you an answer to why children learn more effectively and - what we adults can learn from them. For more than twenty years I have been dealing with this question and have found many interesting backgrounds that I would like to share with you ..."

In this case, the speaker succeeds in briefly outlining the topic on the basis of a simple personal story. This form of introduction is easy to understand and clearly illustrates how a suitable introduction to a speech can be designed. It also highlights a connection with the audience ("what we adults can learn from them"), which proves to be a great advantage when it comes to an introduction. The speaker clearly shows the audience that he wants to help the audience with his speech.

Restrict yourself to the essentials

In the introduction it is probably most important that you align all your statements in such a way that they all lead to the topic. In the beginning there is no room for long excesses and unnecessary delays that distract from the essentials.

The listeners have gathered for a certain reason - they want to gain new insights, be convinced of something or appreciate an event. If you start your speech by focusing on something completely different, you will quickly annoy your audience and lose their trust and attention in just a few seconds.

Therefore, be clear in your remarks and explain precisely to your listeners why it is worth listening to you. You have something important to report, let your listeners know. Humor, emotionally charged images and words, creativity - just a few ideas to draw attention to your cause.

But please always keep one thing in mind: You expect attention? First give your listeners what they expect from you. This as a rule involves knowledge and mental impulses, occasionally also emotional words. That is why you have to show right at the beginning what you (and your speech) have to offer. Embrace the audience's interest and hold the audience's attention.

And one more thing: Be enthusiastic. Speak passionately. Especially in the beginning, this is your chance to win people over to you and your cause. Your audience will be like you and will be infected by your enthusiasm for the subject.

The Main Part

The main part primarily deals with the presentation of the core statements. Depending on the occasion and type of speech: Sharing information, revealing opinions, presenting evidence, examples and comparisons, visualizing models, explaining concepts, analyzing problems - basically everything that constitutes a speech.

Creating a meaningful subdivision

The main part is the longest and most detailed part of the speech in terms of content and time. Therefore, it makes sense to subdivide it. The subdivision into individual parts can be carried out according to logical, psychological or chronological aspects.

In brief: A logical outline aims at the objectively correct representation of factual aspects, the psychological outline is more focused on tension and intensification, while a chronological outline represents the chronologically correct order.

However, it has been proven that it is wiser to restrict oneself to a maximum of two approaches in the structure. For good reason, the most popular variant is the logical-psychological one.

The combination of logical structure and a rising tension during the speech is easy to implement and easy to understand. In addition, you secure the attention of the listeners by structuring your thoughts in an orderly way and building up additional tension.

Examples of suitable speeches

In the following I have selected from a variety of possible outlines those that have proven to be the most promising methods to give your speech a meaningful structure. A structure that, of course, aims at constructing statements and arguments logically on the one hand and to build up tension at the same time. The following outlines take both into account (if you do it right).

Please note, however, that these outlines, which are described in this chapter, only apply to the *main part*. In addition, the introduction and conclusion must always be taken into account!

Structuring the main part

- Yesterday -Today – Tomorrow

- Objective - Planning - Execution - Control

- From Simple to Difficult

- From Individual to Whole

- From General to Special

- Cause - Effect – Solution

- Pro - Contra – Conclusion

- Actual vs. Target Analysis

- Problem - Cause – Solution

- From Beginning until Today

Explaining all the different sections of the speech in detail would go beyond the scope of this book. However, I would like to present one of the variants to you. This speech formula, which I will describe in more detail, is one of the most effective from the list and is therefore most frequently used.

Yesterday - Today - Tomorrow

One of the simplest ways to give a speech a meaningful structure is the speech formula *yesterday - today – tomorrow*. This structure is especially helpful for beginners. The simple structure is also particularly suitable for spontaneous speech opportunities and is exemplary for the other speech structures that are conceived according to the rule of three.

- **Yesterday**

  History: What happened yesterday? First tell us how something began and developed, what you experienced or what obstacles and successes you encountered along the way.

- **Today**

  Actual situation, problem: You then discuss the current situation and describe, for example, the status of a project, the revenue situation of your company or upcoming tasks.

- **Tomorrow**

  Possible solutions, outlook: A glance at the future will round off your speech: What will be tomorrow? Where do you want to go? What do you want? What do you demand or recommend?

Due to its simplicity, this speech formula offers a great advantage for you as a speaker. You can express your opinion in a structured way without having to worry about adhering to the order. It's not even necessary. This also makes it easier for the listeners to follow your words and, in case of doubt, you can even gain time to formulate the whole thing elegantly.

As a beginner you will be able to gain initial experience with this proven and idiot-proof concept and even to revert to the *Yesterday-Today-Tomorrow-Formula* in spontaneous, unprepared situations.

Also characteristic of this speech formula is that it can be applied to the other speech structures included in the list. This means that if you prefer to rely on the Cause-and-Effect- model for your topic, you can easily use the example mentioned above as a reference. The model shown here serves as a template for all forms and formulas of speech.

The Conclusion

You must never underestimate the conclusion and should therefore proceed with caution. After all, the audience will remember the end of the speech very well. At the end, you as the speaker will take stock, summarize and round off the statements of the main part.

How to conclude a speech successfully? Since there is no standard rule and you can (and should!) be particularly flexible in this respect, I have compiled the best possible options for you:

- **Establish a connection between the contents of the main body and the conclusion.** Ideally, you can "move forward" even further and refer to the introduction, if you have set up a thesis at the beginning and answer it at the end. Or you have left a story open at the beginning and can reveal its outcome at the end - as long as it fits the core statement of the topic.

- **You are welcome to conclude with an appeal to the audience.** As a rule, however, this only works in persuasive speeches if you address the sense of justice or responsibility of the listeners, for example. As a result you turn your message into an effective and memorable imperative. And if you actually mobilize your audience to take action, your reputation as a speaker will increase enormously. In this case, you are then regarded as a true doer who motivates people and makes the impossible possible.

- **Complete the speech with a quote.** That's my personal favorite: A quote at the end is always suitable because it will almost always complete the speech excellently and add significance and emphasis to your message. Choose a suitable quote from a personality who is best known to the audience. Of course, also name the author of the quotation! At the end, you can earn valuable bonus points. The more popular and admired the personality, the better for you. For it is you who will be associated with the personality and for whose words you will ultimately be celebrated by the audience.

- **Properly used, humor is a perfect stylistic device for speech.** This is especially true for specialist lectures that demand a lot from the audience in terms of content. When the audience laughs at the end of the speech, they leave the lecture with a good feeling. What could be better for a speaker? But be careful: you must have a good sense of humor and act confidently on stage.

- **The opportunity speech often expresses good wishes for the future of the honoree.** An invitation to all people present to participate in a joint action (glass lifting, minute of silence, celebration) is also customary. This signals our being conscious of ourselves and at the same time acknowledges the occasion, which is ultimately the purpose of an occasional speech.

Nevertheless, I would like to provide you with a few general recommendations: For example, it never does any harm to summarize the essential contents of the main section. The audience will then be able to better memorize what has already been said and keep the information in their minds for a longer time. Especially when dealing with complex topics, it is essential to summarize the key statements at the end.

But keep the closing statement short. Similar to the introduction, you must not digress at the end of your speech, otherwise you will lose the attention and goodwill of the audience. The conclusion must not contain any new arguments or new examples. Work here exclusively with what you already have, anything else would devalue the previous content and weaken your presentation.

So if you are already on the home straight, make sure you keep moving forward. Once the listeners have noticed that you are heading for the end of the speech, their concentration will increase again. Take advantage of this! Conclude the speech with memorable words and make your point of view or the core statement of the speech once again clear.

I would like to give you an extra tip: *Never* thank the audience for their attention. At the end of their performance, inexperienced speakers often thank the audience for their attention. But why should you thank the audience? After all, you are the one who prepared yourself for days or even weeks, went on stage and created great value for the audience.

The audience should thank you. How would you feel if a popular rock band explicitly thanked you for your attention at the end of their concert? The perceived competence drops to sixth-grade level. Such a phrase is uninspiring and demonstrates a lack of professionalism. Just keep it simple and say thank you, if necessary.

And finally ...

Be creative at the end. Feel free to link some of the above-mentioned recommendations and conclude your speech impressively.

You don't have to burden your listeners with incoherent supplements at the end. Simply concentrate on finishing your speech without much spectacle by harmoniously rounding off the content and paying attention to simplicity. Once the audience understands the conclusion, they usually understand the message and core statement of your presentation. Therefore, keep the conclusion as short and concise as possible. Brevity is the soul of wit!

The Right Balance

"What is the right relationship between introduction, main part and conclusion?" is often asked. The relation between the three parts should roughly look like this:

i)   Introduction: 10 - 15 %

ii)   Main part: 75 - 80 %

iii) Conclusion: 5 - 10 %

The introduction can also be shorter when giving occasional speeches. For factual and persuasive speeches, however, this is the optimum balance between the three parts of the outline.

3 Parts - Speech Outline: Structuring the Speech

The Introduction

The introduction serves to establish contact with the listeners and to arouse the necessary attention. It should introduce the topic in an elegant and understandable way, without the actual content being dealt with.

In the case of persuasive speeches and lectures, the introduction includes...

- **the welcoming and salutation of the audience,**
- **an inventive opening sentence,**
- **the thematic introduction of the audience to the main section.**

In occasional speeches, the occasion is usually mentioned immediately after the salutation.

Otherwise, think up an inventive introduction that corresponds to your topic and catches the audience's interest. Describe briefly what your presentation is about and restrict yourself to the essentials. Show the audience that you have come to impart knowledge and provide solutions to their problems. The introduction should be easy to understand and clearly presented.

The Main Part

The main part is about conveying all content and all statements in the clearest possible way. You should keep the goal of the speech in mind and head for it. The details count in this context, so use examples, models, graphics, comparisons (depending on the form of speech), and explain them in detail so that the connection to your topic becomes clear. Nevertheless, keep the big picture in mind.

(Summary)

Since the main part is usually relatively long, it makes sense to subdivide it. Choose a concept that fits your speech intention and supports the speech goal from a logical and psychological point of view.

It is best to proceed in such a way that a certain order is recognizable in your thought process and that you build up additional tension. The audience prefers a speaker who provides a clear structure in his line of argumentation and at the same time makes it easy for the audience to pay attention.

The Conclusion

You can proceed flexibly at the end of the speech. Quotation, appeal, humor - there are several possible ways for you to finish your speech optimally. There are a few basic things, however, that should be considered.

Among other things, a summary of the essential core statement(s) is always an advantage. The audience then keeps your most important message better in mind. Don't introduce any new aspects, just address what has already been said.

You should keep your final statement as short as possible. This will add even more emphasis to the last words, which will have a positive effect on your overall appearance. You are considered a consequent and straightforward speaker if you conclude your speech according to the motto "less is more".

A Proven Strategy:
The Five-Step Formula

The three-part outline - introduction, main part, conclusion - is basically correct and especially suitable as a theoretical model to demonstrate the rough structure of a successful speech to beginners.

But in order to be successful on stage, you need to be more precise and plan the conceptual structure of a speech in detail. A simple division into three parts is usually not sufficient. More importantly, we need a specific formula, a step-by-step plan, in order to shape the speech in such a way ...

- ... that its clear structure **helps the speaker follow the individual steps**,

- ... that the **audience clearly perceives what the lecture is about** and therefore better understands its content.

In order to make this process as transparent as possible, the so-called five-step formula was developed, which has been successfully applied for thousands of years. It is one of the most popular formulas. For simplicity's sake, it is also called a five-finger paragraph structure or five-sentence structure.

The principle behind this is to build up an argumentation step by step so that the listener can easily comprehend each individual train of thought. The essential message or statement of the speech is then presented at the end in the form of a conclusion.

This speech formula is perfectly suited for simple persuasive lectures. However, it can also be used for a factual lecture or an impromptu speech, which makes it so special. For every occasion and every form of speech, the five-step formula offers a convenient template for creating a high-quality lecture. And the overall advantage is that this formula is suitable for all levels of difficulty – for beginners as well as advanced speakers.

The structure is as follows:

1) **Arouse interest**
   Evoke the curiosity of the audience.

2) **Describe the topic of the speech**
   Give an overview of the speech content.

3) **Provide reasons and examples**
   What are the possibilities? What are the arguments?
   What does this mean for the implementation?

4) **Draw a conclusion**
   What are the consequences?

5) **Call to action**
   What is the audience supposed to do now?

The first two steps correspond to the introduction (see previous chapter). The speaker must attract the attention of the audience and briefly describe what the lecture is about.

In this context the goal of the lecture, the speaker's opinion, or point of view, or a particular thesis are expressed. Relatively at the beginning (step 2) the purpose of the lecture is stated, therefore this part of the structure is also called purpose statement.

The third step, *Provide reasons and examples*, represents the main part. You already know this: The essential statements are supported by all kinds of models and tools in order to reinforce the propagated opinion.

After a conclusion (step 4), you can pronounce an appeal at the very end. However, this fifth and final step is rather optional and is only used, if at all, for persuasive speeches.

I advise you to memorize the five-step formula. It is universally applicable, so you can use it anytime and anywhere. This means that you are, so to speak, always "prepared for an emergency" and can deliver a suitable speech at any time, because you have a simple process in mind on which you can rely.

5-Step Formula: A Proven Strategy
(Summary)

The 5-step formula is a meaningful strategy that allows you to clearly structure your speech. This formula is simple and, above all, always applicable, which turns it into a convenient means for delivering a solid speech without much preparation.

1) **Arouse interest**

2) **Describe the topic of the speech**

3) **Provide reasons and examples**

4) **Draw a conclusion**

5) **Call to action**

You only have to follow the individual steps and divide the speech into smaller sections. This considerably simplifies the process of implementation. As a result, you will be able to arrange the big picture clearly and create the conditions for a pleasant experience - both for yourself and for the listeners.

Performing Convincingly and Impressing the Audience

The next chapters will deal with how you exude authority on stage and perform safely. You will learn how to use your body and your voice to be perceived as a competent speaker, how to better convey your arguments and how to select the right statements to win the audience over to your objective for speaking.

7 Methods for a Self-Confident Appearance

The methods described in this section are all of great importance for a confident appearance and should be applied by you if you want to achieve the desired result - a successful speech. That is why I have paid particular attention here to putting practical relevance in the foreground.

This chapter deals with how you can increase your perceived competence through clothing, movement, posture, gestures, facial expressions, tonality and correct positioning in the room, and how you can ultimately appear more convincingly.

As at the very beginning of this book, the methods and tips listed here are applicable to all situations in life, even if we often refer to a particular performance on stage. This formulation was chosen because it is easy to understand and is intended to help sketch a clear picture.

This image does not only imply the typical clichéd stage as we imagine it: A stage-like pedestal on which famous speakers give speeches in front of hundreds of people.

No, the advice in this chapter also applies to everyday life. We always find ourselves in a position where we either have to convince someone of our opinion, pass on information or want to touch people emotionally, whether in business or private life. Just imagine the stage of life when we are talking about a stage. And the stage of life covers everything. And so the methods mentioned here also cover everything you need to know about a self-confident appearance.

Maybe at first you will find it hard to keep an eye on everything at the same time. Nevertheless, please try to include so many of the methods mentioned here in your presentation. The more of it you implement, the better it is for you and your presentation!

1) Choose the right clothes

Before your words are heard, you will be seen. The first impression is crucial because the audience evaluates you and your presentation based on how you look and how you affect your audience. The first and foremost thing we see on a person are his clothes, and we unfortunately judge people by their appearances. After all, humans are superficial. You can't change it, but you can take advantage of it.

Dress in such a way that your clothing matches the topic and represents the message you want to convey. You should also know the clientele, your audience, and their dress preferences. We like it when people behave and dress the way we do. This also makes us more receptive to their ideas, of which we should be convinced.

You speak to a group of managers? Put on a suit or blazer if you want to influence your audience with your speech.

At the same time, however, it is just as important that you feel confident in what you wear - and don't feel compelled to disguise yourself. However, there are a few basic things you should consider when choosing your clothes.

- **A well-groomed appearance is mandatory.** This has always been the case and will remain so in the future. Your audience derives your competence and credibility from your appearance. Therefore: ironed shirt, clean shoes, new haircut - everything looks neat and the size of your clothes fits.

- **Invest in your clothes.** They don't have to be made by the most expensive tailor in town and you don't have to wear luxury brands. However, invest in high-quality materials and make sure that what you wear is of good quality. The audience unconsciously notices this and assigns these qualities to you.

- **Play with the colors:** Depending on the speech goal, it makes sense to choose the right colors for your outfit. Strong contrasts symbolize authority, while simple green and blue tones have a calming effect on the audience. Red colors, on the other hand, stimulate the emotions of the audience. Avoid unusual or even exotic color variations. If you can't make up your mind: In most cases a moderate blue shirt with beige chinos is always a good solution. For man and woman.

If you make the right decisions when choosing clothes based on the above-mentioned aspects, you will be well ahead of most of the speakers and you will collect valuable bonus points from the audience.

2) A Confident Posture is Worth its Weight in Gold

The second thing your listeners immediately notice is your posture, they will judge you by your physical appearance. For our outer appearance reveals what happens inside you. And especially at the beginning it is important to be mentally stable - and also to signal stability to the outside world.

In the first seconds of your presentation, you decide whether to lose your nerve or remain confident. It is therefore extremely important to assume a steady posture right from the start.

For psychological reasons concentrate on performing professionally and on conveying a feeling of security from the start to the end. Do you play to avoid losing? Or do you play to win? It is better to keep in mind the possibility of victory. This will considerably increase your success compared to being afraid of defeats and failures. Develop a winning mentality as soon as you enter the stage. A self-assured charisma then emerges automatically.

The following tips will show you how to ensure a stable posture and position yourself confidently on stage. This advice applies to everyone, regardless of the general attitude towards life.

- **Place your feet hip-width and assume a natural pose.** Don't assume a military-rigid pose, and also don't place your feet too wide apart. If your feet are spread too wide apart, the audience will inevitably perceive it as a sign of arrogance. Find your middle and make sure you keep an acceptable distance between your feet. Watch your balance.

- **Change your posture from time to time.** You are not a tree that has taken root on stage, use the space and move.

- Occasionally, **you can include a casual gesture in your presentation.** For example, you can put a hand into your pocket or shift your weight to one foot. That exudes naturalness. But only stay in this position for a short time, because too much nonchalance can be perceived as arrogant or presumptuous.

Adopt the proper posture right at the beginning of your presentation: Slightly spread feet and a calm, upright upper body with relaxed shoulders are recommendable. Return to this starting position again and again in the course of your remarks.

3) Give Your Audience a Smile

Has it ever been a good idea to go on stage, give a lecture and at the same time pay so much attention to being serious - that you forget to smile?

Who doesn't know them, the stage-droids. In everyday life, ordinary people with feelings, but as soon as they have to give a speech and present themselves, they become expressionless robots whose faces seem to be petrified. Some speakers say that their presentation is so important that a smile or even a sign of emotion is out of place and would jeopardize the seriousness of the speaker.

It is, however, a misjudgement - a fallacy that often proves expensive for many speakers. Who always shows himself on stage with an emotionless facial expression can never fully unfold the power of his statements and doesn't seem trustworthy to his listeners either.

This also applies to specialist lectures. The audience doesn't develop any sympathy for this kind of speaker and in the worst case you sabotage your own lecture.

But it's so easy! With a smile you significantly increase your sympathy points and enhance the formal quality of your presentation. A smile costs nothing and everyone benefits from it. It lightens the mood - which is beneficial for both the speaker and the audience.

Of course, make sure it's an authentic smile. The occasion should be the right one and the timing should be appropriate. Smile only when you think that it is really the right moment, but don't force yourself to smile. Too much of a good thing can actually seem tensed and dubious. You signal sovereignty when you occasionally put on a charming and sincere smile.

Which mimic expressions can you use to create a relaxed and cheerful atmosphere during the lecture? There are some tricks that only a few know, but which are extremely effective.

- **Regular nodding reinforces the positive mood** and can subconsciously trigger feelings of approval from the audience. The universal "Yes"-signal should be used especially during breaks if you want to convince your listeners of a certain statement.

- **Adapt your facial expressions to the respective situation.** If you tell a sad story, it is best to underline it by putting yourself in the right emotional state, and by highlighting the emotion with the right facial expression (and body language). That doesn't mean you have to make faces and become a comedian. Transport your message naturally.

- Similar to the second point, yet worth a mention: **Relax and smile when you report something positive.** But also show grief and anger when your presentation demands it.

- **Show enthusiasm!** In ancient Rome people said: "What you want to ignite in others must burn in you". If you feel passion for your topic, do not hide it. On the contrary: Exploit this advantage, show your passion by using all gestural and mimic means. Then you will arouse this enthusiasm in your listeners. It will be much easier for you than you think. People let themselves be inspired by ideas that are conveyed with enthusiasm.

Even if you now know the basics about the correct facial expressions when speaking in public: Stay true to yourself. Keep it natural and authentic.

I repeat it again: Authenticity is required in this context. And to be credible, you should follow the rules - but not at any price. Better no smile at all than a forced, slanted grin. Honest joy is always better.

4) Make Eye Contact

Especially on stage it is very important to keep eye contact with your audience. This is something with which most people have problems in everyday life anyway. And indeed, it is especially difficult for beginners to face their audience during the lecture. Besides the lack of experience, uncertainty is the decisive factor.

But this also poses a challenge to some experienced speakers. The causes are different (excessive concentration and arrogance), but the result is the same. Without eye contact even the most convincing statements are only partially effective. The word "eye contact" already implies the following: Contact is established between speaker and listener, thus resulting in some important advantages:

▸   The concentration rises on both sides. The speaker acts more effectively, concentrates on speaking and the listeners pay more attention to him.

▸   The speaker demonstrates security and reinforces his verbal statements. The audience responds better to the content.

▸   The speaker learns from the reactions of the audience whether his statements are understood. He also recognizes clues as to whether his speaking pace and volume are appropriate.

However, these worthwhile benefits are only achieved when eye contact is established. But first you have to know how to do it properly. Some people make the mistake of either staring at individual listeners or hectically looking back and forth. Be smart and avoid these mishaps by simply adhering to the following principles when it comes to establishing a meaningful eye contact.

- **Do not start talking right away.** First assume your speaking position and let your gaze wander through the room. As a result, you gain an overview of your audience and the location of the event, which gives you an enormous advantage. (Or do you think Caesar went to war without knowing the enemy and the battlefield?)

- **Arrange your listeners in groups.** These groups could, for example, be front-middle-back or right-middle-left, divided into three to five subgroups depending on their size. A kind of "grid" makes sense in this context. Briefly focus on each group and then move on to the next one.

- **A quick look (three to five seconds)** at the individual groups is sufficient. Do not look at individuals too long. The only exception to this rule concerns opinion leaders and important personalities. They can be looked at in a more sustainable way.

When switching between listener groups, make sure that all listeners are involved. Do not just look at your best friend who is in the audience. Even persons with special status, such as the CEO or the event manager, may not be unilaterally preferred. Make sure that you make eye contact with your audience in a balanced way. A pattern in the form of the letter W, which you can mentally draw through the auditorium and only have to follow, can help.

Of course, all this presupposes that you speak freely in front of the audience. It is a very effective method for a confident appearance, to work without keyword manuscripts and to memorize the contents exactly beforehand.

If you are not yet so advanced and depend on a keyword manuscript, it is advisable to always switch between the manuscript and the audience.

First look at your notes and think about what you want to say about the next keyword; then look back at the listeners and express your thoughts. Exercise first, whether you use a manuscript or not. Training makes perfect and the more often you exercise the lecture, the less you ultimately have to rely on your notes.

5) Use Your Voice Correctly

Our voice is the direct means of transport for interpersonal communication. Not what we say is often decisive for communicative success, but how we say something. The voice probably reveals most strongly whether you are delighted, sad or nervous at the moment.

The spoken word can sound exciting and captivate its listeners or bore the audience to death.

Speech technique is an important success factor for your speech. Speech technique is the term used to describe articulation, volume, speed of speech and pauses in speech, all of which determine successful verbal communication.

Before I go into the details, I would like to point out to you that your voice *is absolutely fine*. Many people are dissatisfied with the sound of their own voice and are almost ashamed when they hear it on video or tape. Almost everyone reacts that way. But it is only the speaker himself who is not satisfied with his own voice. Maybe that applies to you, too.

But I can assure you that your voice sounds perfectly normal, people around you will confirm that. We are simply not used to hearing our own voice, which actually sounds different in reality than we perceive it when we speak. Just accept your voice as it is. The following tips will help you get the most out of it.

- **Speak clearly.** This advice may not be new to you, but relatively few people pay attention to clear pronunciation and precise articulation when they are on stage. Due to their excitement, especially beginners find it difficult to express themselves clearly because they talk too fast. Therefore, speak more slowly than usual to avoid this effect.

- **Vary the volume to express certain statements.** In general, however, you should speak a little louder than normal. Those who speak too softly appear insecure and fragile, but those who speak too loudly are usually perceived as incompetent. Therefore: Speak a little louder than usual and, every now and then, if necessary, softly emphasize individual statements.

- **The speech rate should also be variable.** This may sound like a contradiction to the first point, but it is not. If you are able to articulate clearly even at a high speech rate, you are free to use so-called power talking at certain points. Power talking is about talking powerfully and fast. The focus is on avoiding filler words and speaking as fluently as possible. Sometimes fast, sometimes slow - in the ideal case you change the speed and build up tension.

- **Try to avoid a monotonous vocal pitch.** Highlight individual words by adjusting the intonation from time to time. This is also called voice modulation. This means that you use your voice in such a way that you speak louder, increase the speed a little or adopt a softer tone.

- **Use speaking pauses.** Particularly before your most important arguments, pauses unfold a wonderful dramaturgy and emphasize the content of what is said. Both parties also gain a moment to think about what comes next (speaker) or to process the previous statement (listener).

You convince with a varied voice and are able to emphasize highlights elegantly by unfolding them through the different variations of your vocal organ. Play a little with the recommendations mentioned here! In your spare time you can train your voice and the different speaking techniques excellently, if you are alone in a quiet place.

6) Targeted Movements

Unclear, uncertain movements are the first signs of nervousness. Those who feel insecure express this through their body language. He digs his hands in his trouser pockets, scratches his back of the head in embarrassment and always shifts the weight from one leg to the other.

The way of walking also differs from that of a self-confident personality. Uncertain and nervous people walk slowly and "wander around" because they are simply undecided and this mental attitude is reflected in direction they take.

In everyday life, it is relatively easy to tell from a person's movements whether they are self-confident or anxiously nervous; on stage, this behavior becomes apparent even more quickly.

Make sure that you and your messages are not only noticed but also taken seriously. You probably will succeed best if you exude authentic self-confidence. In this case, it means emitting non-verbal signals. And your non-verbal signals - your body language - should be coherent and support you and your statements in some way.

This does not mean that you have to resort to exaggerated gestures in order to attract attention (unfortunately many think so). On the contrary, simple, precise and targeted movements give weight to your statements.

- **Come to rest and collect yourself** before you set off or start using gestures. You can only use elegant movements and show clear body language when you are at rest.

- **First the signal, then the speech.** Words and gestures run synchronously, albeit with a slight time lag. Always ensure that your non-verbal signs have a small lead over the content, so that you arouse the listener's interest at the decisive moment.

- **Show your palms.** That signals trustworthiness. You have nothing to hide and can therefore gesticulate openly with your hands. You will gain an enormous advantage because the public will trust you much more.

- **Slow movements always prove advantageous.** Not only do the individual gestures become more fluid and precise, the listeners also experience feelings of comfort. With fast hectic movements you endanger the attention of the audience, because in case of doubt you may appear like a puppet. Slow movements, on the other hand, are evidence of dignity, intelligence and seriousness.

- **Determination instead of timidity.** Determined and confident people move very purposefully. You do not have to think up any actions and prolong them unnecessarily. Stop fiddling around in your pocket if you do not want to take anything out of it. And if there is actually something in your pocket you need: Take it out without detours. Your movements are straight and focused!

Body language is like any other language: You do not learn it overnight. And even mere reading will not produce the desired results.

Exercise whenever the opportunity arises and integrate targeted movements into your everyday life. Test the ideas mentioned here first in relaxed conversations at work or when you are together with your friends.

Pay attention to naturalness and try not to appear too motivated. Gradually, if you use the knowledge provided in this book profitably, you will be able to recognize the first positive results and make targeted movements your habit.

7) Make Yourself Big!

This seventh and final method for self-confident appearance deals with two components: Firstly, the psychological aspect. You must mentally take on the role of a strong personality so that you can shine on stage and convince people of yourself. On the other hand, you must also use your body language correctly in order to credibly convince yourself and the audience of this role.

So you have to "make yourself big" in two ways: On the one hand by a self-confident mental attitude and on the other hand by showing physical presence on stage. This method completes the seven practical methods for a self-confident appearance during a successful speech.

So if you are already on stage, then show yourself. You cannot give a good speech and convince the audience if you play hide and seek on stage and make yourself small. You have entered the stage to present yourself and your ideas! Then go for it!

Certainly, it is anything but easy to speak in front of people, especially if there are many people. It is certainly a challenge and requires a lot of courage to go on stage and present something to a large (or small) crowd. The attention of a dozen or perhaps even hundreds of people is solely focused on you for a certain period of time.

Now the crucial question arises: How do you deal with this situation? Our action always results from two motives - fear or passion. You can now be in despair and think: *"Oh no! So many people ... What am I going to do now? I don't want to screw it up ..."*

Such a thought keeps you small. You look at the situation from the perspective the audience against me. The audience is in the majority and whoever is in the majority has the upper hand. But in reality, it is your fear that has the upper hand over you. You can now imagine the worst possible scenarios that will never happen, **or you can change your view of things and approach the matter courageously.**

Your listeners are people like you and me. The listeners have the same problems, the same worries and the same fears as you and I. Or do you think you are the only person on the planet who has trouble speaking to an audience at first? We all have to face this challenge (sooner or later). And this is exactly the point at which we can make a decision.

Either you decide to be afraid of the challenge and make yourself small - or you gather all our energy and your profitable abilities and take all your courage **and ROCK the stage and show the world what YOU are capable of.**

Show the world what you are capable of! You give your speech for the purpose of helping, informing, inspiring and convincing people. And in order to convey the content convincingly, you must be convinced of yourself. Put yourself intellectually into the role of a self-confident and strong person who looks forward to challenges and masters them very well.

But you must also convey this basic attitude with authenticity. Otherwise your whole presentation will come across as artificial. As already mentioned, you have to convince the audience that you are motivated and simply want to give this speech. And that you have prepared yourself for days and weeks to deliver a really awesome result that will provide the audience with an excellent experience.

The side effect of this is that if you move as if you were a motivated speaker who is confident, then you feel the same way. You automatically assume this role, so to speak, if you behave according to the role. And I have a few valuable tips on hand to help you develop this role:

- **Show your body in its full magnificence.** Be energetic and keep your upper body upright at all times. Chest forward, chin up, shoulders backward. Try it out and you will notice how your whole charisma changes significantly in a few seconds. But keep in mind: Your whole appearance should be natural, not exaggerated or tense. Keep this initial form.

- **Take a deep breath.** The psychological and physical effect of deeply relaxed breathing is often underestimated. Breathe in deeply, right into your stomach. You can speak more impulsively and demonstrably have more energy as soon as you start to move.

- **Be well visible - to all listeners.** Position yourself in such a way that all listeners can recognize you well and (theoretically) establish eye contact with every person in the room.

- **Take the entire room.** Assume at least three different positions on the stage between which you occasionally switch during the lecture. In this way you can avoid being rooted to a spot like a tree all the time. Steer resolutely towards the individual points, but move calmly and composedly at the same time. The individual steps take up a lot of space.

- **Fill the room with gestures.** Depending on the size of the auditorium, a distinction must be made. If the audience is small (not more than five people), gesticulate only with your fingers and wrists. A medium-large audience (5 - 10 people) needs gestures evolving from your elbows. A larger audience of more than ten people will require gestures that are more excessive and come from the shoulder joint.

You do not need to jump around wildly or fidget with your arms to show physical presence during the lecture. It is enough to perform resolutely, to accentuate individual gestures clearly and, above all, to show oneself in full size. Show that you are bodily present on stage. Demonstrate your presence!

You use your precise movements and clear statements to let everyone in the room know: *"Here I am and I have something to say."*

Expect attention and respect and you will receive it. Your expectations determine the reactions of the audience. Your expectations determine the result. Expect only the best from your presentation. And you will get the best.

If you do everything right, interpret the recommendations mentioned here and tackle the presentation professionally, the audience will reward you with unconditional attention and maximum respect. And you will reward yourself with a performance of which you can be really proud in the end.

7 Methods for a Self-Confident Appearance

1) Choose the right clothes.

- ▸ The outfit must correspond to the occasion.
- ▸ A well-groomed appearance is a must.
- ▸ Invest in your clothes.
- ▸ Use the right colors.

2) A stable posture is worth its weight in gold.

- ▸ Keep the possibility of victory in mind.
- ▸ Stand with your feet hip-width apart.
- ▸ Change your posture from time to time.
- ▸ Occasionally apply a casual gesture.

3) Give your listeners a smile.

- ▸ Smile if you feel like it.
- ▸ Adapt your facial expressions to the situation.
- ▸ Show enthusiasm!
- ▸ Never show fake emotions.

4) Make eye contact.

- ▸ Firstly, capture your audience before you talk.
- ▸ Group your listeners.
- ▸ A short look at the individual groups is enough.
- ▸ Establish eye contact with the audience in a balanced way.

(Summary)

5) Use your voice correctly.

- ▸ Speak clearly and comprehensively.
- ▸ Vary the volume.
- ▸ Vary the speed of your speech.
- ▸ Emphasize individual words.
- ▸ Use speech pauses.

6) Targeted movements.

- ▸ Relax before you set yourself in motion.
- ▸ First the gesture, then the statement.
- ▸ Show your palms.
- ▸ Slow movements are always an advantage.
- ▸ Pay attention to determined and targeted movements.

7) Make yourself big!

- ▸ Believe in yourself and be motivated.
- ▸ Show the magnificence of your body.
- ▸ Be clearly visible to all listeners.
- ▸ Assume different positions.
- ▸ Fill the room with gestures.
- ▸ **Set high expectations for yourself.**

Arguing Logically -

How to Convince with Factual Arguments

This chapter will show you how to skillfully use factual arguments to give substance to your presentation. Factual arguments form the basis of a convincing speech and should therefore be used in both information and opinion speeches.

Regarding convincing factual arguments you will learn in this chapter how...

> ... to draw comprehensible conclusions,
>
> ... to make use of different sources for a clear presentation of evidence,
>
> ... to convince the audience with an objective style.

The Three Best Conclusions

You can draw three different types of conclusions to convince your audience of a statement. They all lead to a comprehensible argumentation, which seems logical to the listeners at first sight. The good thing about it is that the argumentation seems logical. The statements do not necessarily have to be true, these methods also support untrue or half true statements if you use them correctly.

In a sense, this is helpful because you do not always have to pay attention to sense and nonsense regarding your arguments (but you should), but you can simply assert your opinion or statement.

1) Typologies - clever predictions!

Humans share a very special weakness. We are used to being put into pigeonholes by others - and to putting others into pigeonholes ourselves. This happens mostly unconsciously. Our brain works like this.

This effect is also called *typology*. Typologies are generalizations that explain the world to us and make predictions possible. Usually they are correct and help us understand the world (*"firemen save lives"*), but sometimes typologies can distort our world view because they are too subjective (*"Because he is a hippie, he is lazy"*).

It is precisely this effect that you can trigger in your listeners by describing people on the basis of past events and drawing conclusions for the future that serve your speech goal.

"He has a criminal past and has been in prison twice. It is only a matter of time until he will violate the law again."

"Even as a little child, he was a gifted draftsman. One day he will become a famous artist!"

This sort of argument is easy to understand and appears obvious. Is it the truth? We do not know it, but we believe it.

2) Syllogism - the logical conclusion

A syllogism is a logical argument composed of three parts: the so-called main premise (premise 1), the secondary premise (premise 2) and the conclusion derived from the premises (conclusion: C).

Syllogisms yield statements that are generally valid in a certain situation. Sounds more complicated than it is. Here is an example:

All men are mortal. (1)
Socrates is a man. (2)
→ **Socrates is mortal. (C)**

They prove a thesis, in this case *"Is Socrates mortal?"*, with two successive, irrefutable truths that complement each other. These two statements form the conditions for producing a logical conclusion or for substantiating an assertion. One plus two doesn't always make three. One plus two makes conclusion C in this case!

3) Enthymeme - effective sham conclusions

An incomplete conclusion is called an enthymeme. An enthymeme is a conclusion that does not include all prerequisites, i.e. at least one prerequisite is deliberately left unmentioned in order to strengthen the expressiveness of the argument.

"Only outstanding actors win an Oscar. Leonardo Di Caprio won an Oscar. Which means, he's an outstanding actor."

The probable is promoted to an undeniable truth. Now, who can deny that Leonardo Di Caprio is not an outstanding actor? Even though he has won an Oscar, the most prestigious award for an actor - whether he is an outstanding actor lies in the eye of the beholder and cannot be measured in numbers or other objective criteria.

It is simply an assertion, which is proven by a supposedly objective proof. A proof that is recognized by almost all people! This makes sham conclusions a powerful and versatile method to substantiate theses in a comprehensible way and to convince the audience of false assertions.

Using Sources for Clear Evidence

There is hardly a more effective way to substantiate a statement than by supporting it with figures, data and facts. This creates transparency, makes you appear competent and supports your arguments in a professional manner.

Whoever gives a scientific lecture without resorting to quotations, statistics or research results will find it very difficult to convince the audience with his statements. If not enough information is given, how should a lecture appear serious? Can the speaker then be taken seriously at all?

I don't think so. Therefore it is indispensable to use sources for factual and technical lectures, because only these make an information speech and its contents visible. The listeners mostly want to see hard facts and get clear evidence for certain facts. Also with persuasive speeches one should be able to use different sources for oneself, because also here proofs are in demand.

Many people think that statistical data and scientific studies would "bore the audience to death" and would rather do harm to the lecture. As a result, the lecture would be perceived by some as dull. That is only partly true.

It all depends on how you convey the message and with what motivation you present the source. So two different people can present the same statistics, one will transform it into a vivid diagram and present the findings with enthusiasm - while the other creates a meaningless table of numbers and reads out the individual data listlessly.

Sources can be highly exciting if they are incorporated correctly into the lecture and the information contained therein is put into the right context. The way the source is presented is crucial. You can impulsively pronounce a quotation from an important personality and at the same time skillfully create a link to your main message.

With correctly used and well-presented sources, you can significantly enhance the quality of your presentation.

I would like to encourage you to use the following sources for your next lecture.

1) References - strategies of successful people

References refer to specific facts and methods carried out by role models. You want to draw the audience's attention to a strategy that has already helped successful people (part of a respective industry) to solve a certain problem and wish to explain why this strategy is also a possible solution to your audience's problem.

> *"Warren Buffett, the world's most successful investor and America's second-richest man, has recently revealed his greatest investment secret in an interview. According to Buffett, the most important thing to bear in mind when making an investment ... "*

> *"The decisive success factor for Italy's World Cup victory in 2006 was team spirit. The players had a tremendous team spirit and could thus turn into an unbeatable unit on the field. The same applies to companies ... "*

References can also be used in a negative sense. This means that if there is a certain strategy that inevitably leads to failure, you can also refer to such negative examples in your lecture to warn the audience of problematic strategies.

2) Statistics - numbers do not lie

Statistics have a *tremendous* advantage - they represent the truth in the form of indisputable numbers and facts. For every listener, a statistic is at the same time proof of a certain fact, because it reflects the past and the present numerically and draws conclusions for the future. It is difficult to refute them. And hardly anyone takes the trouble to check statistics as to their truth content, because for humans numbers represent reality.

Since statistics are often compiled by experts and recognized organizations, they are an excellent means for the speaker to support his statements with clear facts and to give the presentation as a whole a more professional character.

Or would you as a listener come up with the idea of questioning official statistics from the Federal Ministry of Economics and Energy?

"As reported by the Federal Statistical Office, 4.3% fewer start-ups were reported in Florida this year than in the previous year."

How you proceed with this information is up to you. You can use the information to derive a thesis from it that worries the audience...

"For the first time in more than thirty years, the number of start-ups in Florida has declined compared to the previous year. This can't be good!"

... or trigger the opposite reaction in your listeners:

"Measured in absolute figures, with 37,000 official business registrations, the number of start-ups in Florida is still very high. There's nothing to worry about."

A single statistic never shows the whole truth! Only several data form the overall picture. And you can choose which facts you mention and which you don't in order to support your statements in the best possible way. For this reason, it can be a huge advantage to include statistics in your presentation.

Those who know how to use them correctly can present their statements in a comprehensible and transparent manner. And ultimately win the audience over to their own convictions.

If you want to use statistics in your presentation, it is best to use this template:

(I)   State the name of the scientist/institution

Who compiled the statistics?

"The famous US psychologist Paul Ekman stated ..."

"According to the Federal Office of Transport and Digital Infrastructure ..."

"The Education Foundation has found out ..."

(II)   Briefly outline the essential information

What is the main message of the statistics?

"... that people find it hard to understand their fellow men."

"... German manufacturers of automobiles have set new sales records."

"... that the number of university graduates has increased dramatically."

(III)   Specify the source, if available

Where can I find the information? Was there a contractor?

"In his book 'Emotions Revealed' he writes ..."

"The annual report of Company A revealed ..."

"A study was conducted on behalf of the Federal Government ..."

(IV)   Present the result as clearly as possible

What can be presented?

"... that more than half of all humans misinterpret emotions."

"... that 15,000 more cars were sold in the last quarter."

"... that the number of university degrees increased by 22 percent."

(V) Draw a convincing conclusion

What's all this about?

"The misinterpretation of emotions can have negative consequences."

"The future prospects of the German automotive industry are great."

"The rising number of academics is an example of the knowledge society."

The purpose of a statistic in a lecture is to draw conclusions from it to support your core statements. In this way, statistics become relevant for a lecture. If you use statistics incorrectly and simply read the numbers out, you will not inform the audience adequately and lengthen the presentation unnecessarily without giving any content.

Use statistics to derive smart insights and enrich the speech with interesting facts. Therefore, it is necessary to present the facts vividly and to convey the statements contained therein in a comprehensible way.

3) Quotes - Wisdom can work wonders

"A good aphorism is the wisdom of a book in a single sentence", Theodor Fontane once said. And those are quotes: They allow you to elegantly summarize complicated facts, and give a touch of elegance to a statement.

It costs nothing to find a suitable quote. Certainly, there are experts in your field who deal or have dealt with your topic. And their views on the facts can be useful for your presentation.

We have already examined the effect of quotations. They make difficult issues look simple, add elegance to a statement and put the speaker in a better light, provided they are popular personalities.

No special knowledge is required to select the right quotation and integrate it optimally into the presentation. You have to do some research until you find the right quote and then place it in a meaningful context.

In the case of an informative lecture, it should of course be an acknowledged expert - a luminary in his field - who is quoted. Let yourself be guided by your feelings when you think you have found the right one.

In the case of factual arguments, you should structure quotations according to the same structure as you do with statistics. The five-step template from the last chapter can help you. If you use a quote from an expert, explain the meaning and - as already mentioned - introduce the author of the quote beforehand. And last of all: Always quote literally.

How to Present Factual Arguments Correctly

Get the emotions under control!

Factual arguments live from the fact that they are presented in a *factual* style. Quite a few speakers make the following mistake: They are unable to suppress their feelings when they present a topic that is important to them.

Avoid this mistake. You put yourself on the spot when you get emotional about factual arguments. This will dilute your conclusions and thus devalue the entire lecture in a rather unpleasant way - because an all too sensitive appearance usually sabotages the comprehensibility of the facts and also seems highly dubious.

Always keep your mission in mind: you want to convince the public of your opinion by objective means. And not trigger feelings.

Knowing when enough is enough

Provide as many arguments as necessary. If you continue to present one argument after another after you have convinced your audience, your audience will feel persuaded in the end.

The tragedy is that you already had your listeners on your side. But since you couldn't put a stop to it, you lost them. A guiding principle helps you prevent such situations:

Don't finish your speech if you can't think of any more arguments. Finish your speech when you have presented all the important arguments.

Observe the reactions in the audience and stop convincing when you have already achieved your goal.

The best comes at the end

Save the strongest arguments for the end. You already know - people don't have the best memory. That's why the end always sticks in our heads.

If you bring out the heavy artillery right at the beginning, only the weak arguments remain at the end and you can at best pass on a few insignificant thoughts. Make it smarter and increase the quality of your arguments during the speech. With increasing suspense and ever-increasing power, it will be easy for you to convince your audience on an objective level.

Arguing Logically: How to Convince with Factual Arguments

The Three Best Conclusions

1) Typologies - clever predictions

Use typologies to describe people and predict their future behavior based on this description.

2) Syllogism - the logical conclusion

From two prerequisites for an event you derive an easily understandable conclusion. Well suited to answer complicated theses easily.

3) Enthymeme - effective sham conclusions

You make an assertion based on what appears to be an undisputed fact. This fact is not measurable, but depends on whether it is recognized by the audience or not.

Using Sources for a Clear Presentation of Evidence

1) References - Strategies of successful people

References refer to specific strategies and methods that have been carried out by role models. Using a reference is always an advantage, especially if you offer solutions to your listeners.

2) Statistics - Numbers do not lie

You can use statistics to present interesting facts in the form of numbers. Present the facts clearly and professionally. Always deduce a conclusion from the statistics shown!

(Summary)

3) Quotes - Wisdom can work wonders

Find an expert who has already successfully dealt with the topic you introduce. The opinion of a renowned expert will always enrich your presentation, regardless of whether or not you agree with him.

How to Present Factual Arguments Correctly

Get the emotions under control!

Remain objective. Even if the topic is important to you, you have to behave professionally. This is only possible if you keep a cool head and have your feelings under control.

Knowing when enough is enough

Provide only as many arguments as necessary. Don't finish your speech if you can't think of any more arguments. Finish your speech when you have presented all the important arguments. Keep an eye on the reactions of the audience.

The best comes at the end

Save the strongest arguments for the end. Increase the quality of your arguments in the course of the speech and think carefully in advance which argument comes last.

Triggering Emotions
How to Win the Heart of the Audience

Why are athletes, musicians, actors and writers famous and successful? Quite simple: Their performances arouse feelings in us. We are happy when our favorite club wins an important soccer game and that's exactly how we grieve when our serial favorite has to die.

And this is exactly what distinguishes the mediocre speakers from the successful ones. If you want to become a successful speaker and win people over, you have to trigger feelings in your audience. And that is exactly what this chapter is about.

You learn ...

> ... **how feelings emerge,**
> ... **what kind of content you can use to arouse feelings,**
> ... **how to act when you present emotional arguments.**

The Origin of Emotions

Everything we do and everything we don't do originates from two motives. Either we act out of fear, or we act out of passion. We want to avoid suffering (motive of fear) or strive for joy (motive of desire). Each of our decisions depends on whether our fear of suffering defeats the desire for joy or vice versa.

Your life is the sum of all the decisions you have ever made. Did you focus on security? Or was it more important to you to do what really satisfies you?

In any case, you have developed a certain system of values for yourself. Think of it as a priority list: The most important thing for you is probably your own survival. What comes after that varies from person to person:

Personal success, strong friendships, fun and enjoyment or the well-being of the family belong to the most important priorities. And this is where emotions interfere. When we look at the world, we see either that the existing conditions are optimal to meet our needs, meaning our values are safe. Then we have positive feelings. You don't say "the world is fine" without a reason when you're well. But if something is wrong and our ideal world is threatened by something, we quickly experience fear, anger or frustration.

That's exactly what speeches can trigger. A speaker can either touch people and show that everything is wonderful and pacify their world view or frighten his listeners because their world is in danger.

"Why should I trigger discomfort in the audience?" I'm sure you're thinking now.

Well, there are good reasons to sometimes bring your listeners into a state of fear. If you want to warn against careless decisions and encourage the audience to act accordingly, for example.

Don't forget: Your goal is to use arguments to convince people of your statements. Factual arguments are intended to reach the listeners via their minds, just as emotional arguments are intended to win the hearts of the listeners. Both ways serve to motivate the audience to act or to adopt a certain view of the world.

When using emotional arguments, you should always trigger the feelings that serve your speech goal. And these can also be feelings of fear and anger, which ultimately make the listener believe your opinion.

Emotional arguments through aversion (Unwillingness to suffer)

Or the avoidance of the bad. Here you specifically address the fears of your listeners because you want to convince them of an action that prevents suffering. You point out unpleasant events in the past and draw parallels to the present and the future to warn against the same mistakes.

For example, you can name your own negative experiences, those of the listener or third parties. You can also simply envision a worst-case scenario.

This is not about the negative experience itself. Rather, it is your goal to awaken negative feelings in the listener and trigger in him the desire to get rid of them by taking action and doing what you say.

Example: In the Ministry of Defense of the Republican Union there is a rumor that the Communist Federation is in the process of developing a very dangerous special weapon. The commander takes the floor.

"We just can't sit here without doing anything! The Communist Federation is about to develop a weapon that will ruin us all. If we don't get our hands on their plans and have the special weapon before they do, we will have lost. Do we want to see our beloved ones dying because we have been hesitating? We must immediately send a spy to get us the plans and then promptly start the construction of this weapon!"

Emotional arguments through appetence (desire for joy)

In other words also the desire for good. You try to seduce the listener and entice him to do something he enjoys. Assume the role of the motivator, one that puts the audience in ecstasy and promises only the best. Because what he promises would mean pure happiness for the listener. And who does not like happiness?

Soccer Cup Final. It is the prestige duel of the two best teams in the country. At halftime the score stood at 1:1. The head coach uses the break to give a speech in the dressing room to motivate his players.

"Well, guys, go out and play the best 45 minutes you've ever played. I want each of you to fight to the end. Think of the reward, the trophy you'll be holding in your hands! Think of the fans who will call your names and cheer you! You have the unique opportunity to make yourself immortal and

celebrate the greatest success of your career if you win the game. Go out and win! Glory will be ours!"

Imagine both scenarios in as much detail as possible. The more vivid and dramatic the image you convey, the more you will influence your audience with your words. You convince your listeners all the more when they develop strong feelings and feel compelled to act.

Convincing with the Right Content

Which sources can you use to best convey emotional arguments? There are three very good methods that trigger emotions in the listener. I would like to introduce these to you.

1) Examples - experiences are based on true events

Humans are compassionate beings. We strive to make others feel as good as we do. At least most of the time. That's why we're all the more upset when something bad has happened to others. So examples work particularly well with emotional arguments of aversion, that is, when we draw attention to tragic fates.

These may have happened to ourselves, to a listener, or to someone else. As you already know, what counts is not so much the event itself or the person to whom it happened, but rather the feeling that the example awakens in us.

But of course it can also be positive experiences that you report about. Examples can either refer to you, to one of those present, or to a person who is not present. The focus is always on the fact that the events described are based on true events. If you let a listener speak for himself, it's like winning the lottery.

Imagine speaking in front of a group of people and trying to convince them to buy an insurance policy from you. Suddenly one of the listeners gets up and tells the audience how this insurance saved him from financial ruin and what a relief this has been for him.

In such a case, you have actually already won. You don't even have to wait for your luck, you can either engage someone in the audience to play this role for you or you can ask the audience something like: *"Who has ever had such an insurance?"* And then continue: *"Who would like to report on his experiences?"*

As a rule, you get what you want: A perfect example of a listener who supports you in your persuasion work. Even if he reports negative experiences, you have a joker (*"And has anyone ever had positive experiences with such an insurance?"*).

If necessary, you can then use clever factual arguments to point out the advantages of your product, which suppress negative feelings and calm the audience.

However, I recommend that you start with your own examples and those of third parties before using examples from the audience. This is a safe and sustainable way to learn to work with examples.

2)   Stories - windows to the past

Since the beginning of the history of mankind, we have loved to tell each other stories.

Whether fairy tales, historical stories or the summary of a novel or a film - stories, if told properly, have an outstanding effect. They are both entertaining and educational, they convey values and norms. People are born and die sometime, but it is their stories that outlive them - us - and make them immortal.

It is the stories that usually show people the right way. Children, for example, do not learn moral values through blunt instructions such as *"Don't do this"* and *"This is wrong"*. Children learn best through stories what is right and what is wrong. It is often fairy tales, stories and anecdotes with which one finds the way into a person's heart, whether young or old, and thus ultimately influences them.

There was once a little dog in India. He walked around and entered a room in a palace with mirrors all around.

The dog faced a large number of strange dogs, the challengers made him angry and he began to bark. Everyone barked back, which made him even angrier. Since none of the strange dogs gave in or surrendered, the little one barked to the point of complete exhaustion and eventually collapsed dead.

Years later a dog came into this mirror room again, he was overwhelmed by the large number of playmates, began to wag his tail and was delighted that even the strange dogs were so happy. The dog went away enriched by a pleasant experience.

The secret of a good story is its liveliness. Use stories for your presentation only if they are told vividly and the message behind them is easy to understand. Above all, you can enhance your audience's sympathy and, of course, convince the public of your opinion if you present a story in a credible manner.

3) Jokes - who laughs, wins

With humor you will gain access to the hearts of your listeners. If you make your audience laugh, you will usually succeed in convincing them of your views. You will achieve much more with your speeches if your listeners like you. And the easiest way to do that is to make them laugh.

We learn to appreciate people especially when they trigger something in us. In particular, when they evoke feelings of joy and love in us. And the same goes for speakers. One of the characteristics of a truly extraordinary speaker is that he inspires people by amusing them. Be that speaker! Be someone who manages to touch people with the right words because you make them laugh. Only very few people can. A well-placed, nice joke makes all the difference. A single joke can turn a dull lecture into a small celebration of joy.

Of course, it takes a bit of exercise and experience until an inexperienced speaker embraces the art of humor and begins to incorporate jokes into his speeches. But it is better to start early rather than hesitate for a long time. The key lies in action! The sooner you start, the faster you will gain experience and the better your jokes will be. The excuse *"you don't have a sense of humor"* doesn't count.

How can you improve your "humor skills"?

First, create a humor collection. Search for good jokes, funny stories, cheerful facts, anecdotes and quotes. Assume a cheerful mind. Put yourself in the role of a creative speaker with a strong sense of fun and joy.

Just imagine being humorous! And exercise in everyday life. Try to make as many people as possible laugh today(!). Every person you have made laugh is a small success, a success that will make you grow and make it easier for you to make your audience laugh later on stage.

Anyone can be humorous if he wants to. Sourpusses are just sourpusses because they have made it their business to spoil everything. But sourpusses are not popular contemporaries and certainly not good speakers. A sourpuss will hardly ever be able to convince people for himself, because he does not radiate enthusiasm. You know, people love to get excited about something.

Therefore, strive for the role of a humorous person who manages to inspire, amuse and delight his fellow human beings. For those who succeed in making people shine will always achieve what they want, because they know how to convince others. And at the end they will win the hearts of their fellow human beings.

How to Effectively Communicate Emotional Arguments

As the name of this chapter suggests, emotional arguments are primarily concerned with the how. How can you communicate emotional arguments correctly and convincingly? Stories, examples and jokes are only good if they are told vividly. Only the right narrative technique allows emotional arguments to be expressed and gives the audience the feeling that they are confronted with a credible speaker.

There is a formula to construct emotional and humorous stories based on mere facts. This is the so-called *surefire storytelling* formula. It is a proven system to build effective emotional arguments.

Proceed as follows (as an example):

1. When

Once upon a time...

1,200 years ago ...

Last month ...

Yesterday ...

2. Who

A prince and a princess ...

The Prophet Mohammed ...

A loyal customer ...

My daughter ...

3. Where

In a distant kingdom ...

In Arabia ...

In the office ...

At my house ...

4. What

Immortally in love ...

Founded a world religion ...

Told me about a movie ...

Played a board game with me ...

This formula is a good basis to introduce stories and jokes that emotionally capture the audience and strengthen your position. As you see, it is just about answering the four W-questions in the right order.

Feel the emotion you want to trigger in others

I'm well aware that I have emphasized it a couple of times in this book. But I really want you to understand and apply this advice, especially when it comes to emotional arguments. You have to feel the emotions yourself that you want to trigger in the audience.

Those who put on a poker face on stage cannot convince their listeners with emotional arguments, even if they produce the best stories and the most interesting examples. Even if they follow the surefire storytelling formula and tell the whole story well, they won't succeed. Simply, because most people notice when a speaker performs in an artificial way and does not "believe" in the message.

And for this reason, it is important that you feel yourself what you want to trigger in others and that you show your feelings! This does not mean that you collapse crying or that you euphorically scream until you turn red. You should rather represent feelings on a professional level. How does that work? It's simple.

Just imagine experiencing the stories you present, with all five senses. You describe every detail and every aspect - without losing sight of the essentials. You see a clear picture in front of you, hear the voices and ambient sounds, feel the atmosphere of this place at a particular time and smell, taste and feel the surroundings and the events you present. Pick up the mood and reproduce it as well as possible!

It sounds bizarre at first glance, but believe me, it will work. If you immerse yourself into the time and the place of the event and tell the story (or anecdote) vividly and convincingly, you will take your audience with you on this journey and trigger the same feelings and impressions that you experience. Your perceived credibility is multiplied by a factor of ten, at least.

Feel the moment and your listeners will sympathize. Then you have won.

Triggering emotions:
How to win the hearts of your audience

The Origin of Emotions

All our actions are based on two motives: the unwillingness to suffer or the desire for joy. It makes sense to trigger one these emotions in the audience, depending on what you want to achieve with your speech.

Emotional arguments through aversion (unwillingness to suffer)

You focus on the fears of the audience because you want to convince them of an action that avoids suffering.

Emotional arguments through appetence (desire for joy)

They arouse the listener's desire for a feeling of success, love and happiness. You want to get the audience to do something that pleases them. The stronger the emotions you trigger in the audience, the more likely it is that the audience will be convinced of your message.

Convincing with the Right Content

1) Examples - experiences are based on true events

Use examples from real life that are based either on your own experiences, those of the listeners, or those of people who are not present.

2) Stories - windows to the past

Use fairy tales, historical stories and short stories to convey a specific message. Stories are vivid and that's exactly why they are so suitable for triggering feelings and spreading ideas.

(Summary)

3) Jokes - who laughs wins

You will win the hearts of your audience if you make them laugh. You will also convince the audience of your opinion if you occasionally include a well-placed joke in your presentation.

How to Effectively Communicate Emotional Arguments

Always introduce stories with the surefire storytelling formula (When, Who, Where, When). This narrative technique is proven and transforms facts into emotional arguments. In addition, you form a solid foundation on which you can establish those emotional arguments.

Feel the emotion you want to trigger in others

Express feelings as to what you say and show them. It is only then that you will appear credible and your message will be accepted. Narrating stories, or jokes requires that you put yourself in the situation in which they took place. If you report as pictorially and vividly as possible, then you will convince your audience sustainably.

Let's Get Started!

In the last chapters you will find specific instructions on how to plan your speech properly and how to deliver it successfully. The chapters will also address common problems and provide you with the best way to deal with them. Here you will learn how to work out a successful speech. At the end, you will also get a few last tips.

10 Steps: From the first idea to the final speech

"A journey of one thousand miles begins with the first step."

Chinese proverb

If you want to speak professionally, you have to prepare yourself like a professional. The first step to a successful speech is a successful preparation. Proceed systematically and follow the structure below.

10 steps from the first idea to the final speech

1. Set target
2. Write down first ideas
3. Collect material, research
4. Create an outline
5. Prepare the main part
6. Intro and conclusion
7. Prepare media
8. Create a manuscript
9. Rehearsal
10. Let's Get Started!

The individual steps are explained in detail on the following pages. Use the structure as a guide.

Step 1: Set a target

You must have a goal in mind if you want to achieve something. By the way, this applies to all areas of life, especially to speeches and lectures. Before you ask yourself how to deliver a speech, you must answer the question why. Why are you going on stage? Why are you giving a lecture on a specific topic? Why do you want to talk?

If you have clear answers to these questions, success will occur automatically. You will be able to easily remove obstacles and master your presentation with high probability. The why is always your strongest weapon on the way to a successful speech. Those who know their reasons and have a clear vision in mind will always achieve their goals. Of course, this presupposes that you also pay as much attention as possible to the further recommendations here in the book.

Once you have identified your why, all you need is an idea of what you want to achieve with your speech. Consequently, it makes sense to deal with the occasion first. So the goal can be either informing, persuading or inspiring (or all at once). Have a look again at the three types of speech as they are described at the beginning of the book. Then form a suitable general idea that permeates the entire lecture.

Establish a concrete schedule to determine when and how much you will work and set yourself a deadline in writing by which you must complete your preparations at the latest. Also write down which of the ten steps you need to perform on the respective days and by when which sub-goals need to be reached.

Step 2: Write down your first ideas

Next, you should define a topic. A topic that interests you and helps you achieve your goal. It is advisable to think about it (in time!). Whether you are driving a car or taking a shower – start thinking at an early stage about your topic, the content and the focus.

Especially at the beginning of your preparation, you will spontaneously have the one or other good thought, which you may not be able to implement immediately. Therefore you should write it down. You should definitely record your thoughts on paper so that you can work with them later. Otherwise, you will forget a good idea, which would be a shame, because a good idea rarely emerges a second time.

So have a piece of paper ready right at the beginning that is intended for writing down sporadic ideas. Whenever a good thought comes to you that might be useful to your speech, write it down as soon as possible.

With this simple and yet extremely sustainable method, you make sure that no idea gets lost. You will be grateful when you will have a wealth of ideas and a pool of creative inspirations to work with later on.

Step 3: Collect material, do research

You won't be able to make everything up on your own, and you shouldn't either. You have to resort to content and sources in order to give your presentation substance. And that must not be any content and sources. It must be the best content and sources you can find!

Unprofessional speakers pay little attention to the quality and seriousness of the sources on which they ultimately base their presentations. They simply take the first material without investigating more precisely. Please do not misunderstand me, any source is a good source if it is properly integrated into the lecture.

It is always a great deal up to the speaker himself how he works with the existing material and what he makes of it. But those who base their knowledge only on average sources, such as most Internet articles and YouTube videos are, will never be able to really go into the depths of content and thus only scratch the surface.

In particular, make use of specialist books and journals, read current daily newspapers when they deal with your subject, browse for scientific research and studies, go to the library or company archives and talk to experts and those who have already mastered similar things.

Also take a look at older speeches on your topic so that you can learn from them. Build a wide range of many different sources and collect as much information as possible. By the way: The more you know, the safer you will feel on stage later.

Step 4: Create an outline

Make an early effort to develop a clear structure for your presentation, the sooner the better. You can thus shape your work much more effectively and concretize the contents at an early stage by deepening thematic focuses in good time and sorting out useless aspects of your work. In addition, you can see from a first rough outline whether you may need further materials. This saves time and energy afterwards.

The best way to do this is to read the chapter **Structuring the Speech** again and then immediately look at the **Five-step formula** to get an overview of what an outline should look like.

Step 5: Work out the main part

All your important thoughts and ideas flow into the main part. All important thoughts and ideas do not mean all thoughts and ideas. Only extract the essential points that really need to be said.

It often happens that speakers acquire a lot of expertise in their field and overload the lecture with it. They overload the lecture with complicated expressions and difficult details. Remember, the audience is not at the same level as you. Thoughts that you take for granted are new to the listeners and must first be processed by them.

Therefore, you need to communicate the content to your listeners in an understandable way, without appearing educational.

Understandable means explaining the subject in such a way that on the one hand the thought processes are well structured and on the other hand few technical terms are used, and if they are used, then only followed by an explanation.

Communicate only what is absolutely necessary and have the courage to leave out certain aspects that may deviate too much from the actual topic or go into too much detail.

In the main part, it is crucial to present the big picture in a simple way and to go into depth at individual points. With regard to informative speeches: Give your listeners the feeling that they listen to an expert who turns them into experts themselves.

By contrast, with regard to persuasive speeches, imagine that you are a large fire that ignites small fires (inspires its listeners).

In other words, you have to deliver the right degree of information so that on the one hand every ignorant person is immediately in the picture and at the same time the experts in the audience can learn something new.

And when it comes to opinion speeches, your goal is to inspire the already enthusiastic even more and at the same time win over the greatest critics to your side. Difficult, but possible! In the main part, it's all or nothing.

Step 6: Formulate introduction and conclusion

First plan the main part, then the beginning and the end? Yes, that's right. Of course, you can also proceed differently in your preparation, but I clearly recommend the variant described here. Once the main part is finished, it is far easier to think about a successful introduction and a suitable conclusion, simply because you have created a foundation on which you can rely.

This also ensures that you don't reveal too much at the beginning (many shoot their powder right at the beginning) and that you don't add additional information or throw in new arguments at the end.

You already know the scheme: At the beginning you should arouse the interest of the listeners without revealing too much and the end of the speech is aimed at rounding off the lecture. In both cases, it is necessary to limit oneself to the essentials and not to present statements that are intended for the main part.

Step 7: Prepare media

Now is the time to support your statements with some kind of media. This step is optional. However, media are a good means to make your content clear to the audience using several senses (seeing, hearing, smelling, feeling).

A powerpoint presentation, a short video clip, or an audio recording can be used. Perhaps you would like to present a prototype or let the public touch your latest product? Basically all means are allowed which help you accompany and underline your words on a visual, auditory and/or tactile level.

Make sure that you get these media in time. A Powerpoint is not created overnight (and if it is, it will be pretty bad in most cases), and preparing a short film takes longer than most people think. So make sure in a timely manner that you involve your media as early as possible in your preparation and have enough time to design them professionally.

Step 8: Create a manuscript

It is not difficult to create a good keyword manuscript. If only most of us knew how to do it. It happens to many speakers that they plan every single word of their presentation and stick to them. The manuscript resembles a continuous text that is simply read. The whole presentation then appears unauthentic, unprofessional and insecure.

The other extreme is made up of people who don't take notes at all, try to memorize everything and then start to speak freely - in my opinion the better idea, but also not a very good one. Because once you lose the thread - which often happens because of the excitement - things can get critical. Then you stand there, on stage, and you just can't remember what you wanted to say.

Therefore, it is advisable to find the golden mean. Prepare a keyword manuscript that really consists of keyword-like notes and memorize them as much as possible. It's not mandatory to remember everything written on the paper. It serves you more as a safeguard.

Just keep the essential content in mind. You don't need to read anything and can fully focus on the audience.

You simply think of what you have written on your piece of paper and establish eye contact during this time. And if you should actually lose the thread, you can simply look briefly at your notes and quickly locate the thought again (which would not be the case with a continuous text).

In this way you kill two birds with one stone: you can speak freely and are prepared for emergencies.

Step 9: Final rehearsal

It goes without saying that you should rehearse your speech at least once. However, there are some things you should be aware of in advance.

Take the final rehearsal seriously. Many only rehearse half-heartedly, which then leads to problems during the performance and often ends in unpleasant situations. The better you prepare and the more intensively you study the lecture in advance, the more amazing the results will be. Act as if you are already on stage and proceed professionally, especially during rehearsals.

My experience has shown that it is best to deliver your speech in front of other people. These can be friends, family or colleagues. This gives you the opportunity to get honest feedback and optimize certain things.

Let's keep in mind that the actual work is done behind the scenes. If you train hard and get the best out of yourself while practicing, the lecture will be easy for you. That doesn't mean you have to overdo it. If you study the lecture three or four times, it will be sufficient. Anything else would be negligent (bad or completely unprepared) or an insane waste of time (too many rehearsals).

Step 10: Let's get started!

Now the time has come. You will soon go on stage and present what you have been preparing for for days or even weeks in just a few minutes. Do you already feel the excitement rising inside you? That's the way how winners feel!

Unfortunately, many speakers tend to be overly nervous before the performance, which is reflected in the performance and destroys even the best preparation. Of course, I can't say something like "keep cool" or "take it easy" right now.

Because even the greatest and most experienced speakers, including myself, always feel a certain excitement before the performance. But this excitement can turn into a big boost if you handle it right.

It is important that you don't get stressed. Therefore, you should again be aware of your motivation and motives. You have come to win, haven't you? You are going on stage because you want to deliver a great speech to the audience and to go beyond yourself. You have come to show what you are capable of and what a great speaker you are.

You need to regain confidence before you go on stage. Take a deep breath, imagine the best possible scenario, tell yourself that you can do it and that you are ready for the challenge (go to the bathroom first!) and focus on your self-confidence and charisma. Then enter the stage. You will make it!

10 Steps: From the First Idea to the Final Speech

Step 1: Set the target

First find your why. Why do you want to give a speech? And what's the occasion? Which form of speech (information, persuasion, inspiration) is suitable? Once you have answered these three questions, proceed to the planning stage. Determine exactly when you do what and which steps are implemented when.

Step 2: Write down your first ideas

Now choose a suitable topic and write down new ideas every day. Record your thoughts on a sheet of paper. In this way you collect a lot of good ideas, which can later prove to be extremely valuable.

Step 3: Collect material, do research

Find good sources on which you can base your lecture. This can be technical literature, but also real experts are always a good solution. Make sure you also take a look at older and current lectures on your topic and learn from them.

Step 4: Create an outline

Create a meaningful structure right at the beginning of your preparation. This makes your work easier because you can proceed in a more targeted manner and sort out superfluous material.

Step 5: Work out the main part

Work out the essential content and formulate your most important statements and arguments. In the main part, you should make sure that you present the big picture in an understandable way and that you go into the depth of the content at individual points.

(Summary)

Step 6: Formulate the introduction and conclusion

Concentrate on the essentials. At the beginning, the listeners decide whether you are worth their attention, and at the end, they reassess how good your presentation was. Therefore, plan the introduction and conclusion in such a way that you arouse interest at the beginning and round off the content at the end.

Step 7: Prepare the media

All forms of supporting media can help you to elegantly "spice up" your speech. You should take care of them in time. Also make sure that everything works properly. Plan and test the workflow before using media.

Step 8: Create a manuscript

Prepare a keyword manuscript consisting of short notes and memorize it as much as possible. A good keyword manuscript is advantageous in two ways. It lets you perform confidently on stage and provides security in difficult situations.

Step 9: Final rehearsal

Exercise your lecture well. Imagine yourself standing on stage. Present your speech to your partner, friends, relatives or acquaintances. In this way, you receive support in advance as well as valuable suggestions for improvement, which can make a decisive difference.

Step 10: Let's Get Started!

Sharpen your senses before you enter the stage. Take a deep breath. Strengthen your confidence by realizing that you are a winner and will master the speech like a winner. Believe in your success.

3 Difficulties and How to Overcome Them

Many speakers suffer from stage fright. Sometimes this also concerns the professionals. There are also other problems and fears that need to be tackled.

So this chapter is about ...

... how to deal with stage fright before and during the speech,

... what you can do if you get stuck or misspeak,

... how you react to rude and disinterested listeners.

How to Overcome Stage Fright?

Stage fright when talking is one of humans' greatest fears. There are not only a few people who suffer from stage fright. On the contrary, I am firmly convinced that it is due to evolution. No one ever born thought: *"I am going to give a speech now. Best in front of a few hundred people."*

Stage fright is a basic fear, just as it is a basic fear you feel when you face a lion in the wilderness. And just as it is possible to tame a lion, it is possible to control stage fright and eliminate this fear.

The best way to overcome speech anxiety is to talk. The more often you speak in front of people and groups, the more normal you will perceive the situation at some point. For this reason, mere reading of this book cannot lead you to success - you must also act. You need to train, train and train it again - and when you think you have trained enough, go on stage and give a speech.

By the way, there are three means to attack your stage fright.

1. Constant training

2. Preparation of your speech

3. Behavior during the speech

Exercise before it gets serious

Look for opportunities to take the floor. Below is a list of possible situations in which you can demonstrate your rhetoric skills.

- Use all possibilities offered by the **company, the family or the group of friends** to raise your voice and give little speeches. These can be short statements during small talk at work or everyday stories that you share with your friends. Try to speak as professionally as possible even on these smaller occasions and apply the tips provided in the book.

- **Speak at each meeting and participate in discussions.** Smaller contributions are the best training method to master speeches. Meetings, for example, are an excellent way to express and argue your opinion.

- Occasionally, **you can act as a moderator** who welcomes guests to celebrations or toasts someone at a family celebration.

- **Visit public events and express your opinion** if the opportunity arises. You will also get used to the atmosphere and the feeling of speaking in front of strangers.

- **Exercise even when there are no listeners around.** The training alone can be supported and enhanced with video recordings or tape recordings. In this way, you learn to use your voice and body language more effectively and check yourself for possible mistakes, which you can then eliminate.

Be aware that all these training situations consist of small speeches. As a result, you will perceive the " real " lecture, which you will give one day, as something normal and approach it in a more relaxed way.

In addition, you will also improve your speech technique, your persuasive powers and your negotiating skills in everyday life, which will be very profitable for you in all areas of life. Fortune favors the doer.

A good preparation ensures your success

There are only a few speeches that arise spontaneously. In such a case, you will have to deliver them off the cuff. In the majority of cases, however, you will have enough time to prepare your speech. You will know well in advance when you will give a speech and how much time you will have to prepare yourself.

This also applies for most of the examples presented in the previous subchapter. It is rather a question of time management. You will need sufficient time to prepare your speech and to acquire a certain level of knowledge.

▸ Start preparing your speech in time and plan carefully when and which tasks you will perform. Thus, you prevent stress and may even have time to allow yourself one or two days off.

▸ Create a reliable keyword manuscript that supports you in tricky situations.

▸ Deliver the speech to friends, family or colleagues who will give you feedback by controlling your content and rhetoric.

It's like an exam at school - the better and more intensive you prepare, the more confident you feel during the exam and the more likely you are to achieve a good result in the end.

Behavior during the lecture

Also during the lecture you can use some methods, which have proven successful to combat stage fright. These are simple manners that help you limit your excitement to a natural level.

- **Rely on your good preparation.** Everything that is important is either anchored in your head or noted on your cue sheet. After all, you are the expert who has prepared for the speech for days or weeks - the audience usually doesn't even know a fraction of what you've learned over the years. Keep that in mind.

- **Believe in your abilities.** You have already mastered many challenges in life. This speech is another element contributing to your positive development.

- **Focus on the big picture and not on details.** In this way, you avoid overestimating trifles and marginal errors, and you also think less about difficult passages and possible problems. What counts is that you present your topic as a whole properly and assert your concern.

No matter what happens: Just go for it. Don't think too much about it. Go on stage and perform as perfectly as possible. Don't judge whether your performance is good or bad. The only thing that matters is that you go for it and that you dare to speak in front of people and grow beyond yourself.

Regardless of how your speech will be perceived by the audience: You can only win. The speech will either be a great success or you will learn from your mistakes and make it better next time.

Tips if You Get Stuck

Another fear that many people like to imagine is to lose the thread during the lecture.

The scenario usually looks like this:

At the rehearsal everything was still running smoothly and during the speech you stare at the keyword and don't know what to say about it. An embarrassing silence spreads across the lecture room and the longer the situation lasts, the more nervous the speaker becomes ...

There is always a certain danger of getting stuck. This is also the main reason why many speakers are afraid to make use of keyword notes and therefore prefer reading a finished word-for-word manuscript to free-speaking. It doesn't have to be! Neither the silence, nor the reading aloud.

Certainly, no one is immune to a blackout. Even the most skilled speaker experiences moments in which he simply can't think of what he actually wanted to say. The question is not how to avoid it. A normal person does hardly manage to learn everything by heart. Rather, one should learn how to handle it professionally and how to solve such blockades skillfully. Just like professional speakers do.

And there is also a proven technology that is very easy to use and can even be used by the top speakers, if they don't know how to proceed at all.

The flow of speech

If you ever forget an argument or a fact, it's no big deal. Since you cannot forget the main message of your entire speech (it is simply impossible not to keep the core idea in mind), it will probably only be a side aspect of your speech anyway, which remains un-mentioned.

It would be much more annoying, however, if you remained silent in front of your audience for half a minute and the beads of sweat began dripping from your forehead. And that only because of a secondary statement, which is not even so important!

So it is far better and more important to maintain your flow of speech than to just add another point of view.

Repeating what has been said

Maintaining the flow of speech is most effective when you return to and deepen the last spoken thought. How's that?

You simply repeat it in other words and gain time to rearrange your thoughts and thereby gain a certain security. The repetition should of course be skillfully and inconspicuously formulated, so that nobody notices it.

Background knowledge required:

"We should deepen this last thought once more."

The classic one:

"Let me sum up what I have said."

Dull, but effective:

"This statement requires a more detailed explanation."

Attention of the audience guaranteed!

"At this point I would like to briefly stop again. This statement is important to understand the big picture."

Questions to the audience

Of course, you can also ask the audience a question and switch from monologue to dialogue. The active exchange of ideas with the audience can sometimes have a stimulating effect on the atmosphere in the hall and open up new perspectives.

In case you want to give examples:

"Have you had similar experiences?"

Simple statements:

"Shall I deepen what I have said?"

Complicated statements:

"Any ambiguities?"

It is of course better to ask open questions in order to avoid yes-no answers. Encourage your audience to think. This ultimately secures your audience's participation because it increases personal interest. Your listeners will even become active helpers!

A Slip of the Tongue? Don't Worry!

Slips of the tongue happen to everyone every day. So don't apologize if a sentence comes across your lips in a clumsy way. Often the listeners do not even notice the slip of the tongue, and only the apology attracts inglorious attention.

If you have the feeling that you were understood despite the slip of the tongue, just consciously ignore it. Simply continue speaking at the same tempo and with the same tone of voice.

In case of a distorting slip of the tongue that has made the sentence incomprehensible, proceed as follows. You only repeat the last sentence using the correct wording. Perhaps you can even turn the slip of the tongue into a little joke and laugh briefly about yourself.

The audience then laughs automatically. We all love people who don't take themselves too seriously and can laugh about themselves. So a slip of the tongue can be your chance to quickly and easily gain more sympathy points.

Interjections and Other Disturbances

However, it is more difficult to deal with disturbances emanating from the audience that negatively affect your speech. Even the best preparation is no guarantee that everything will run smoothly.

It can never be ruled out that one or the other idiot is among the listeners and causes trouble by interjections. It can also happen that individual listeners suddenly leave the hall.

Of course, these can also be factual interjections, of course. And sometimes guests who leave the hall have personal reasons why they have to leave all at once in the middle of a lecture. The question is, how do you deal with it?

There may not be a universal recipe to tackle interjections and disinterest, but there are some effective methods.

Three types of interjections

In principle, each interjection is a disruption of your presentation. However, it is still necessary to determine the type of interjection so that you can react correctly in every situation.

- A factual interjection that supports your statements and contributes to the solution of the problem. **(positive)**

- A heckler, who deliberately wants to disrupt your presentation. He deliberately wants to upset you. **(malicious)**

- A joker, who craves for attention and hopes to get it with unobjective interjections. **(nonserious)**

Dealing with factual interjections

Objective interjections usually have a good and a bad side. A good one, as it gives dynamism to the lecture and requires an active audience, which proves that the listeners are interested.

At the same time, you need to act flexibly. You must react objectively to the interlocutory question and at the same time ensure that you do not deviate from the essential and that you do not give the rudder to the listeners. You should therefore try to answer factual interjections as briefly as possible and at best postpone them to the end.

▸ **Answer factual interjections immediately**, if possible in just a few sentences. You can integrate them directly to deepen statements or clarify ambiguities.

▸ **Postpone the answer to the end of the lecture** or to the subsequent **discussion round**, in case a factual interjection calls for a more detailed answer. This will ensure that your speaking time is not compromised.

"Thank you for your valuable advice! We can talk about this later."

"That's a good point. Please remind me as soon as we enter into the discussion."

▸ Point out that you will discuss this aspect at a later stage if a listener asks a question that you **intend to answer anyway** during the speech.

"This is quite an interesting point of view, which I will discuss in more detail."

▸ Postpone the answer to a later stage and point out that you will answer the question in a **personal conversation** after the presentation if the interjection is irrelevant to the content of the presentation and the audience is not interested.

"I would be happy to discuss this question in a personal conversation after the lecture."

▸ In case a question arises that is of importance and of interest to the audience, but you don't want to answer it immediately, please ask the attendee to **repeat the question**. You gain time for the answer and usually get a more detailed, precisely formulated question.

Dealing with unobjective interjections

Unobjective interjections arise from two motives, as we already know. The troublemaker either wants to consciously disturb you or simply wants to satisfy his urge for attention.

How do you react to something like this as professionally as possible? It is important that you do not show any weakness and at the same time do not get involved in the matter.

Do not under any circumstances engage in discussion with the troublemaker or try to expose him. On the contrary, show by a sovereign reaction that you are above his level.

You can proceed as follows:

- ▸ **Deliberately ignore disturbing interjections.** Pretend like nothing has happened and just keep talking. Some troublemakers are already satisfied with simply getting rid of their contribution.

- ▸ **Ask the troublemaker to stop his interjections.** Do this politely and raise your voice a little bit. Speak as briefly as possible.

"I kindly ask you to stop your interjections. Thank you."

- ▸ **Go on the offensive if the troublemaker does not keep his mouth shut.** Silence him with a direct announcement. Act like a strict teacher and create a silence that makes you appear dominant. After all, you have silenced your opponent. With this method you can really destroy annoying intruders.

"You back there. Do you have anything to say?"

"I'm afraid I don't understand you very well. Can you repeat your interjection?"

"You're welcome to join me on stage and tell the audience what you know and I don't."

However, make sure that you generally pay as little attention as possible to the disturber and grant him as little time as possible.

Otherwise it may happen that he "takes over" your lecture because you concentrate too much on him and not on your content. Eliminate interference briefly and definitely by using the above examples.

Listeners seem to be disinterested

What to do if the listeners visibly lose interest and turn their attention away from you?

It happens every now and then that listeners look out of the window, look at the clock or talk to their neighbour. If it's a few, it's no big deal. Some that can't be enthused are everywhere. Don't let this confuse you and just do your thing.

Check, however, whether you may be exceeding the time limit or digressing too much from the essentials. If this is the case and the number of distracted listeners is increasing, you better head for the end soon. It is better to omit a point of view than to overstrain the patience of the audience.

Listeners leave the room

Even if individual listeners leave the hall, it does not mean that you or the quality of your presentation are in any way to blame.

Sometimes it is a personal need, an urgent call or simply a feeling of unease that makes the listener "turn their backs" on your speech and go home or elsewhere.

Just keep that in mind when it comes to this situation. There can be a hundred reasons why a listener suddenly leaves the room.

Therefore: Stay calm and keep talking.

3 Difficulties and How to Master Them

1) How to Overcome Stage Fright?

The best strategy to fight stage fright is to train in everyday life. If you frequently speak to people and groups, you will get used to the situation at some point. Therefore, take every opportunity to speak and work on your speaking skills.

Exercise before it gets serious

▶ Use all possibilities that arise in the company, in the family or in the group of friends, to raise the word and give small "speeches".

▶ Take the floor at each meeting and participate in discussions.

▶ Visit public events and express your opinion.

▶ Train even if there are no listeners around.

A good preparation ensures your success

▶ Start your preparation in good time.

▶ Create a reliable keyword manuscript.

▶ Give the presentation to friends, family or colleagues.

Behavior during the lecture

▶ Rely on your good preparation.

▶ Believe in your abilities.

▶ Focus on the big picture and not on details.

(Summary)

2) Tips if You Get Stuck

Everybody makes mistakes. You can discreetly conceal them by using proven methods.

The flow of speech

If you ever forget an argument or a fact, there's nothing to worry about. It is better to leave one aspect unmentioned than to create an embarrassing silence. So keep your speech flowing.

Repeating what has been said

Consolidate previous statements and reformulate what has already been said. You gain time to rearrange your thoughts and avoid unpleasant pauses of silence.

Questions to the audience

Ask the audience a question if you should forget your text. This ensures the active participation of your listeners and gives you a short moment to remember your actual message.

A slip of the tongue? Don't worry!

Slips of the tongue are normal. That is why you should face them calmly and not attach any importance to them. Just keep talking like nothing has happened.

If, on the other hand, the statement has become incomprehensible due to misunderstanding, simply repeat the statement.

3 Difficulties and How to Master Them

3) Interjections and Other Disturbances

You should wisely deal with interjections or other disturbances from the audience. Professionalism and composure are required here. Don't get upset and don't get sad or upset right away.

Three types of interjections

1)   The factual-positive interjection: The listeners support your statements and ask constructive questions about the content.

2)   The intentionally malicious interjection: A troublemaker has come after you and wants to upset you.

3)   The unseriously foolish interjection: One of the listeners suffers from an acute lack of attention and wants to attract attention.

Dealing with factual interjections

Try to answer factual interjections as briefly as possible and postpone your answers to the end of the presentation.

Dealing with unobjective interjections

Don't show any signs of weakness and don't become too involved. Don't argue with the troublemaker and don't expose him. Stay confident and demonstrate strength. Pay as little attention as possible to disturbers.

(Summary)

Listeners appear disinterested

There will always be people whom you will not be able to convince of yourself and your cause. When individual listeners get bored, it's no big deal. Focus on those who appreciate your message. But also recognize the right time to finish your lecture otherwise too many people will lose their interest in your speech.

Listeners leave the room

There can be a million reasons why a listener suddenly leaves the room. Just relax and continue talking.

3 Last Tips for Your Success (Outlook)

You now have acquired all the necessary knowledge to become an excellent speaker. You have access to information that the greatest speakers in the history of mankind have already used and thus become very successful.

But for this success to happen, they had to make experiences - experiences that were not always marked by success. Often great personalities had to suffer setbacks and bitter defeats in order to become who they have become.

Success may be what we strive for. Success brings recognition, respect and money. But only our failures let us grow. We can only learn by making mistakes.

Failures, mistakes and setbacks make us stronger, because they provide experience. And it is experience that leads to better decisions, which in turn leads to new successes. Failures are therefore at least as important for our development as successes.

Don't be afraid of mistakes. You'd better be afraid not to make mistakes. Dietrich Bonhoeffer said: *"The biggest mistake you can make in life is to always be afraid of making a mistake."* If you don't suffer setbacks and make mistakes, you deprive yourself of your chance to learn and develop. Failures and setbacks indicate that someone tries to improve, to expand his skills in order to celebrate successes one day. And such a person will be successful. I can guarantee it.

Whoever gets up more often than he falls can be counted among the great and successful, among those who change something on this planet and further develop humanity. For such a person develops himself and learns from his mistakes.

Don't be afraid of mistakes.
Regard mistakes as a chance to learn and grow.

But as soon as the first successes come along, you will celebrate. Success is there to rejoice and enjoy the moment.

This may sound a like a contradiction to what I have said before. But look at it this way: To be successful, it needs self-confidence. And you will never be able to gain lasting self-confidence if you concentrate too much on your failures. Learn from mistakes, but concentrate on your successes.

After all, the way to a happier and more successful life is to concentrate more on what is positive and to capture beautiful experiences. Run a positive memory management and focus on what you have done well and what you are proud of.

Write down your successes. This will extend the period of time you remember it. Think about your outstanding achievements more often and you will find that successes occur more frequently in your life. Greater successes. Outstanding successes.

The more and more intensively you prolong positive thoughts and feelings, the better your life will be. You will achieve more. You will do more of what satisfies you and what you enjoy. You will increasingly improve because you constantly develop your self-confidence and always celebrate new successes.

Your quality of life will improve if you learn to respect yourself. Be proud of what you do. And do more every day than you did yesterday. Success depends on being renewed again and again. And we live from celebrating new successes.

Concentrate on your successes.
Be convinced of your abilities and strengths.

"Rome was not built in one day." Important things need time to become important and the same is true for humans. We need time to develop and become who we want to be.

Be aware that success does not happen overnight. This means that you will not become a great speaker overnight and you will not change your communication significantly overnight.

If you work a little bit on yourself and your communication skills every day and get a better every day, you will wake up one day and see that you have achieved something great. Everything in life will add up.

One day you will discover that the months and years of work have paid off. You will look in the mirror and see a person in front of you who does not only successfully communicate, but also convinces, impresses and affects people.

But it begins with the decision, the decision to act, the decision to venture something very few before you have dared.

How many people do you think are willing to go on stage and deliver a speech? Only a few take responsibility. And how many people do you think are willing to work on themselves, to learn, to improve their skills, to grow beyond themselves? Only the fewest are willing to change themselves and strive for success.

Consider yourself a winner, a winner who is willing to venture great things and outdo himself. Because that's what you are. You belong to the few who want to change something in their lives for the better and therefore have read this book.

If you apply what you have read, you will be richly rewarded. I can promise you that. I wish you only the best and much communicative success on your way to achieving this goal.

No guts, no glory.

3 Last Tips for your Success (Outlook)

1) Do not be afraid of mistakes.

See mistakes as a chance to learn and grow.

2) Concentrate on your successes.

Be convinced of your abilities and strengths.

3) No guts, no glory.

You are destined for greatness.

Acknowledgements

I hope this book will help you become a great speaker. It is the result of passionate work and many personal experiences, experiences that were also based on setbacks and we're not always marked by success. But, as you know, without failure there can be no success! And I think that this book has become a success - thanks to the people who supported me.

Special thanks to my editor, proofreader and friend Antonio Lavento, who proofread this book and eliminated all errors. Thanks to his expertise in terms of content and language, his committed work and friendly support, the book has become what it is - a small masterpiece.

To a great extent I also have to thank my mentor, business partner and manager, who has made a significant contribution to the success of my books. It is his merit that you are allowed to hold this book in your hands. I consider myself infinitely lucky to be able to work together with my role model and to help countless people to improve their lives through our joint work.

I would also like to thank my family and friends, who believe in me, and the success of my books. It is they who drive and inspire me to grow and develop.

Notes

Your BONUS: **A Free e-book!**

I would like to thank you for choosing one of my books and for supporting me and my work. My analysis and discussion of various topics aim at supporting you in changing something in your life - for the better, of course.

As a thank you will receive an ebook from me - completely free of charge! With the help of the ebook *CHARISMA* you will learn how to increase your charisma in a playful way by just following 7 simple steps - at the same time you will develop a strong self-confidence.

My exclusive gift to you:

Free ebook "CHARISMA"

Get your ebook now:

bonus.julius-loewenstein.com

Contents of the free ebook by Julius Loewenstein:

- **The secret of charismatic people**
- **How to control thoughts consciously**
- **The power of words and how to use them**
- **The 4 keys to strong self-confidence**

This offer applies only to those who have already purchased a book by Julius Loewenstein. I would like to delight my readers by giving them this ebook as a gift. Discover the secret of charismatic people. Become an appealing personality with a self-confident charisma in just a few days!

Download the e-book now!

bonus.julius-loewenstein.com

CHARISMA:

How to increase your charisma by following 7 simple steps and develop a deep self-confidence

Made in the USA
Middletown, DE
03 July 2020